T0344553

ART

IS MORE

J.L. SIESLING

To Quinten, Flore and Philémon

(Walt Whitman)

"...to have great poets,
we need great audiences..."

(Charles Bukowski)

"...to have great audiences,
we need great poets ..."

Contents

PART ONE

PART TWO

Preface

At the origin of this book there was an introductory course of art appreciation for American undergraduate college students, now taken out of print. Traces of it are visible throughout. The text of it was however thoroughly revised, greatly enhanced and totally upgraded, so much so that *Art Is More* must be considered as a new book. Not in the least because increased attention was given to the growing impact of the infinite treasures of Asian and African art. Although the underlying thought as developed here is based on the Western experience of history, these foreign intrusions reflect a modern reality: the convergence of cultures as a typical trait of the future of humanity. All over the body of text doubled in volume. It is a blessing to see that *Art is More* approaches the ideals that were announced but baffled in its predecessor: its format and design, its ethics and esthetics. Photographs are banished now; they won't interfere with the art anymore. The chapters are followed by a shortlist of *Major Works*, the difficult choice of which was in part determined by their easy Internet access. Its size is that of a *pocket* book, it can be carried in a pocket; it is that of a *manual*: it can be held in the hand, like a tablet (be it clay or electronic). Its price converts the whole art concerned public to its target group.

The nature of this book is that of an essay, not of a university thesis. Scholars will scorn the lack of footnotes and bibliography. It was written out of memory on a ship sailing slowly from one uninhabited island to another, far from specialized or any other libraries, notably my own. I have tried to turn the adversity into an ally. My last concern was completeness, my first one was fairness. Names mentioned are never at random, but names omitted probably are. There is of course a life time of reading behind this book and it would have been unthinkable without the countless admired authors in the beloved field of art history and in many fields beyond it, science, history, psychology and not least literature. Specialists will recognize them. However, more than upon reading, it is based on *another* life time of first hand contact with art, with artists and with people visiting museums, monuments and exhibitions. They are indeed the ones this book would like to approach. Footnotes and bibliography would not only be haphazard; they would not be of great use, even contradictory to the unconventional outline of art as proposed here. I had to decide to let the book go without the baggage.

INTRODUCTION

About this book...
and how to appreciate it

This book is about art.

About the visual arts and sometimes about architecture. Not the performing arts, poetry, music or even film.

About *immutable* (in the sense of *non-moving*) art objects and our appreciation of them.

This book has a different approach than most others: It is *personal*. Since art appreciation is in the end an individual experience, the author won't make an exception for himself. But the reader will learn what *personal* means in art or history.

Now the discussion can start.

At first glance, art seems simple. It attracts you.

It seems to come toward you: a photograph, a drawing, a sculpture.

It is the other way round, of course. It is you who goes toward it: a flower or a gun, a nose or a nipple, a king or a queen, or just some red or blue. You can't escape its attraction. Inevitably, if you are intelligent, the moment comes that you need to say something, tell the reason why you were attracted, and that is not so easy. You have no words for it. So you say "amazing" or "cool" or "fun," words that mean nothing really. From that moment on, art loses its evidence. And most people turn away from it, thinking it is not for them. Art, however, is not difficult, but rich and complex. That is to say, it has many layers of meaning. One, at least, is for you, or about you; it is probably not the one you see first. Art is as complex as the man or woman who views it. Art tells you as much as you can say about it. The key, the code, or the clue to art is not in the art but in you. So you have to know yourself, if you want to know art. And art will tell you who you are.

If you are someone, you have a history. An art object has its own history. This means that you and the art you look at are determined by different origins: time and place, biology and chemistry, feelings and knowledge. You meet, your histories meet. And you can't help projecting your history onto the artwork. It makes art appreciation subjective.

That is one point, but there is another. You *are* more than your own history; you *are* also the history of many others like your parents and grandparents, your close friends and far enemies, your heroes and your country, and so on. I dare say you are the depository of the history of the entire humankind. Most of it unconsciously, some of it more consciously. We all are. That's why we can learn and even know things we've never experienced. Art is also, in its way, a depository of the history of humankind. Not as complete, but much more visible. Art makes visible what we are. It projects its history onto us. You'd rather look at it with some attention, if you are curious about yourself. If you want to know (and love) yourself, you need to know (and love) art. This makes art appreciation objective.

It brings us to the last point, more difficult, which the study of this book will make clear to you. Speaking of depositories of the past, artworks are made in the long order of time. They represent and embody essential values of the civilizations that have produced them. Civilizations rise and fall, but mankind evolves and discovers itself in ever-growing depth. Civilizations come and go, but artworks stay, like flowers in amber. They transfer the discoveries of humanity about itself from one epoch to the next, and their benefices are not lost for new generations. Compare it to the biological evolution of the species; there is no loss of complexity, but gain of intention or efficiency. We still have a tailbone, and indeed, though we don't swing upside down from a branch anymore, we can greatly enjoy the idea of doing so. A new artwork can't help but store (often invisibly, unwillingly) the properties of all the preceding art periods and then add new ones. There is no way back. We, on the contrary, can only observe (experience) art in the present moment. All art is contemporary to the observer. We must acknowledge that being contemporary is necessary (for us) but not essential (for the work); for the work the source is essential. We have to go down (or up?) to the source.

In conclusion, this is the dynamics of art appreciation: Art goes into the future, while the art lover goes into the past; they meet in the present.

Naively, we say that art is timeless. So are we.

You should begin to understand the starting point of this book: you. Not art. You in your society, your country, your school, your business, your time, your age, your culture. Your society tries to control the arts, to make them fit in its economy. But art, old or modern, seems to rebel. That's maybe why you become curious and turn your eyes in its direction. The goal of this book (or method) is to give you words and categories to think about art with sense; to communicate "with" it; then with others about it; and doing so to give art meaning. *Meaning* is pleasure, or grief, fear or awe, understanding or censure, doubts or security, energy or curiosity, anger or praise and so on. In fact, art gives meaning to you. It is quite certain that you will open yourself to it, like you did for football, web surfing and makeup, skills much more difficult to learn and nobody asked you to do so. If your attitude is right, knowledge comes in by itself. Yahoo, Google, Bing, the Wikipedia (and who not?) will help you . . . until you don't need them anymore. You will learn more and more with less and less effort about art's history and techniques, its forms and content, its value, and its role in our lives. Art could change your life; and you could change the world.

Here is the method.

The book is composed as a series of 35 chapters plus this one. As I said, an art work has layers of meaning. Each chapter deals with a layer; each with a theme or topic that concerns us as human beings in our contemporary and complex society. For instance *Death* is a theme, or *Faith,* or the *Self,* or the *Eye.* The lesson deals with the theme by evoking an art form, an art period, artist, or artwork in which it became (and still is) prominent. The theme or topic is the *source* (of understanding). Now I invite the art to illuminate the topic. But, like a mirror effect, the topic illuminates the art. I do this in general terms, not in details, because more specialized information is to be found with the help of the Internet and the names of major works highlighting the theme at the end of the chapter; they serve as the beginning of deeper insight.

The themes, art forms and art works in this book appear in chronological order. This will give you not only an idea of art's history, but also awareness of the fact that there is a history of appreciation. We don't experience art as our parents. The layers of interpretation (themes) reflect the historical order of their coming into humanity, just like the strata of the surface of the earth a geologist cuts through and reads to know the history of the soil. For the themes that occupy our thinking and constitute our understanding of life there was a moment to enter into the human consciousness and to become manifest (visible) in the arts; then they would never leave. Every theme, once invented, stays present and active in each new (later made) work and later born mind; however, it becomes snowed under the surface by new themes according to the needs of the new period. Inversely, and undoubtedly, new themes may shed new light on preceding works, because the viewer can't help but be the accumulation of all themes prior to his or her own time. Anachronistic reading can give new life to old stones. Put in the metaphor of the river, there is no doubt that the original strength and life of an artwork is to be found in the *source,* though unexpected tributaries will confer new momentum to its stream. However modest, a book like this can only wish to be one of these whirling pools.

Let me give you an example. In a Rembrandt painting, 17th century, the earlier themes of *Death* and *Faith* are certainly present; just as to a greater or smaller degree all the other themes dealt with in the preceding chapters. But the new theme is the *Self,* it lays as it were at the surface and is particularly manifest in the *Self*-portraits; the *Self* is here a source. For the Egyptians, where the source of art centered on *Death,* the *Self* was not yet manifestly in question; I won't mention it. Inversely, the theme of a purely optical approach of reality and art (the *Eye*), supported two centuries later by the Impressionists, was of no concern for Rembrandt. But we may want (in fact can't help) to look at Rembrandt's style with the eye of the Impressionists, because we are born later than both. This may give Rembrandt new and unexpected life; and since the Self did not leave art, it may give greater depth to the Impressionists. However, the greatest satisfaction comes from the source, if we have the courage to go that high up into the mountain of ideas. Rembrandt's *Night Watch* has grown in meaning and depth since the 17th century, but we grow in meaning and depth when we go back to Rembrandt's original challenge.

In the essays I cover subjects of general interest with the help of few severely *selected* artistic events. They are a personal choice; not random, but significant for the composition of the book. I do mention names and dates, but as few as necessary to introduce you to the historical relevance of a topic. These names, as well as those in the ten or twenty works mentioned at the end of each chapter and with more detail in the index, are the starting blocks for beginning art historical research via the Internet and libraries. You know, of course, that you must never trust Internet information (blindly), neither information from books. Trust photographs even less, especially of artworks; that is why there are no reproductions in this book.

This book could have been twice as thick and expensive, or a hundred times, easily. I don't mean that there are innumerable more themes in our lives art deals with than the ones I chose, but I decided to limit the art history concerned by them to the *point of view* that is ours: a global world in the beginning of the twenty-first century with Western Europe and America still in its art historical center. For the sake of its underlying theory, I have funneled the information in that direction. You will keep in mind that the great but foreign traditions of China, India, Africa, Pre-Columbian America, Australia, and many more, even if they fuse today with the Western mainstream, are underrepresented. The more they would be included, the more they would add insight to our comprehension of humanity and the range of art's impact. It must be the object of future editions of the book.

In Part One the lessons invoke cultures or civilizations, wide in area and time, from the Paleolithic era to the European Middle Ages.
In Part Two we confront our themes by a narrow or concentrated approach of the arts: via the bias of a few exemplary artists or artworks, selected from a few Western countries. Here the names of the chapters become art historical vocabulary.

1. What is Art?

How to define it

Everybody asks this question sometimes—young people certainly do—and many think one day or another that they have found the answer. But the question comes back at a new occasion, and a new answer has to be found, radically opposite sometimes, or simply more refined. And so on.

Is that a problem? Well, a valid definition of art would be that it has no definition. Our notion of it changes with us; changes because we grow, move, speak; changes because we change. Not only our general idea of art evolves, also our opinion about a single art piece that we can love one day and detest another.

Art has value, art is value. Values change with life, we have to redefine them all our lives; we define them and they define us.

Us? We? Who am I speaking about? Each of us individually? Yes, you and I, but as members of a group. The definition of art is always the decision (the cohesion) of a group, a community, small or great, family or church, school, state or nation or continent. Art is never isolated. I can, it is true, contest and protest and even refute the group's definition, but eventually I will either rejoin the group or join another. All alone I don't need a definition, my opinion (my "feeling" or my "emotion") is sufficient for me. In fact, my feeling is quite worthless . . . until I am able to share it. I need to discuss it, to defend it, in order to validate it. That is art. It validates my obscure and hesitating intuitions about myself inside the group. The group likes that, needs that, and recuperates its benefits.

The group, let us call it the society. Societies vary, societies change, that is why art varies and changes. The society decides what art is; not the artists. The artists obey, or sometimes they rebel, just like you and me. They usually produce what the society expects from them; otherwise the society would not understand but would reject them. By the way, that happens more often than we think. Societies are not undivided. Their art is not uniform. But unity is what they strive for, also in art, new and old.

The society, in this context called the public, decides what art is. By responding to art, the public *creates* it. That sounds strange in your ears, accustomed to hearing the artist called the *creator*. Personally, I don't use this religious term anymore. The artist is (only) the art's *maker*.[1] She or he is doing the *work*. She or he tries to make the society creative, invites it to call her or his pottering "art," and induces the public to *appreciate*. If the public doesn't, her or his "art" will never be anything but private pottering. Without the society's consent and choice, there is neither art nor appreciation. We understand now why art is not the same in New York, in Mississippi or in Saudi Arabia, which doesn't prevent a Saudi prince from collecting New York art, nor a New York banker to perfectly ignore the art scene of her city.

---

[1] Turning to literature, the English word *poet* comes from the Greek verb *poiein*, which means to do or to make, while *author* comes from the Latin *auctor* meaning not more than "*one who helps something grow*", like a farmer or an educator. An *actor* is also someone who is *doing* a role on stage.

Let me choose two interesting examples to show that a changing society actually shifts what it labels art. In its turn art makes the changes in the society visible for all.

Some five generations ago everybody found children's drawings and paintings ugly and dumb; they were laughed at and put in the trash can (if there was one). *We* think they are beautiful; *we* (or the parents, but also galleries) frame them and hang them on the wall, we treat them as art. Indeed, many artists now paint like children and have their works in the museums. (This doesn't keep one of you from criticizing some contemporary work by mocking that *your little brother* could have done that).

The society, or the public, is slow and inert but not immobile. Sometimes a few artists or poets or critics, pulling like Lilliputians on Gulliver, can make the whole social body move a bit. The second example shows it: African masks. Westerners thought not long ago those masks were savage and unpleasant to look at, good proof of African backwardness. Now we collect them avidly. Only (?) 100 years after Picasso and Matisse, the Metropolitan Museum in New York opened a wide wing for African and Oceanic art, and Paris dedicated a whole new museum to it on the Quai Branly border of the Seine, close to the Eiffel Tower and the Modern Art Museum. Our entire attitude towards Africa or towards our children has changed, and art shows it to us.

We appreciate according to what we *are*. A woman won't appreciate a big stone phallus the same way as a man, even if it is Greek. And even if it is by Michelangelo, a black man won't appreciate a *dying slave* like a white man. We think we appreciate as an individual, but that is an illusion: we appreciate according to one of the groups we are part of, which together form our society. Appreciating is communicating and that is what we have to learn—learn why and how our group appreciates. If not, our appreciation ("feeling") is shallow, a brief satisfaction in private at best.

When you look at an artwork, you *interpret* it, like a musician who interprets the music written by a composer. The musician is not free: the music has its rules and its order. Or like a translator who translates a text into his or her own language; the translator is not free (and the language is not his or her own at all, it's the people's own). Translation, interpretation, comprehension, appreciation, all words that try to describe that communicative (appropriating) activity that takes place in the brain and the body of a human being walking into a temple, a cathedral, a museum, a gallery, an artist studio, an auction room.

Most people think that art's definition begins and ends with the word *beauty*, and in a way they are right. *Beautiful* is the first word in the appreciator's vocabulary. But who tells me what beauty is, the same beauty attracting some, repelling others? Beauty may be in the eye of the beholder, but art is in the mind of the beholder. Anyway, beauty is not limited to art, and beauty is never the core of art. It is rather its *by-product*; a fascinating by-product. Art in the end is about other issues. Artists often don't care much about beauty. They know that art is *more*.

Art is always *more*. More than its appearance, more than matter, more than design. Art is more than the artist, more than form. *Art is more than what the eye can see.* If we accept this as an axiom, we are ready to appreciate in depth. We will experience far more than what we expected. We are not free. But we are what we are, and art will tell us. Art is our freedom.

2. **Art and Humanity**

PALEOLITHIC ORIGINS   ALL CONTINENTS   - 50,000 – -10,000

It is not in a few words that we can define what makes us human, what distinguishes us from the animal. Often we wonder, though, and in wondering we need to know: what is our nature? Here physics, chemistry or biology, objective sciences cannot make the point. We have to search in our past, with the more tentative methods of paleoanthropology.

The essential human trait, then, both for scientific reasoning and common sense, seems to be our capacity to speak. Scholars situate the beginning of the development of human language roughly 50,000 years ago. It is significant that the earliest production of images goes back to broadly speaking the same period. The ear and the eye, two senses, activated by two (much more recent) body functions, the voice and the hand, made our brain human. These four in interaction defined the square that sooner or later allowed the exponential development of the mind. It is reasonable to think that images, however abridged, in two or three dimensions, preceded the words. Whence this elliptic formula: *speech was developed to speak about art*. With help of these faculties, the one interpreting the other, man was able to communicate beyond the limits of his body; he existed in a space where he was not physically present, in a moment that was already past. Human communication tends to ignore the body; it is human to suppose we are not confined to it.

Spoken words and drawn or modeled forms are signs and symbols *all* humans and *only* humans interpret. They are shortcuts to wider meaning. We make the words, but the words make us human.

So does the drawing, the painting, the sculpture: Art makes us human. This is, today in Moscow, Milan, or Mexico City, or 25,000 years ago in Willendorf, Austria, or 15,000 years ago in Altamira, Spain, the deepest truth about art: It confirms our humanity. To our deepest common concern: *Who are we?* or *What are we?* it answers: We are human.

From the start art was useless, or better: it was beyond use. It still is, though societies give it special functions. Why do we need it? We need it in order to be what we are. It resembles us: we know we are more than the tool we use, be that tool a flint stone or a powerful computer. Art was and is the shortcut (symbol, link) to the hidden structure of human consciousness and human desire, which is to be beyond use. Paradoxically, the visual arts show our invisible being.

During some 40,000 years, through natural upheavals like a mortal ice age and most devastating floods, people were able to survive, *painting the animals they were not* and *modeling the women they were from.* Unconsciously they responded to the greatest of all needs: the identity of the species. It is the earliest indication that art expresses our *being* more than our conscious will or thought. The art techniques were sophisticated, but limited in range and very traditional, transmitted from generation to generation. The artistic skills were sometimes unsurpassed. Already there was painting and sculpture as the essential modes of expression. Already they were the strongest markers of their culture and the most eloquent trace that is left. Already the notions of art and craft were overlapping, but not identical. Almost nothing of these remote times is left for us, as Paleolithic people worked mainly in wood, ivory, or bone, easy preys of water and fire. Or they decorated unsteady rock, skins (and their own skins) with vegetal materials the air has made disappear. But some breathtaking monuments are intact, between the Ural and the Atlantic, the greatest known concentration being found on either side of the Pyrenees mountain range. In the eyes of many, the cave of Lascaux in southwest France, not far from the Cro-Magnon cave, conserves the most spectacular one. There, profoundly hidden in the hill, under the level of the soil in a chilly natural dark cave, herds of most powerful bisons and elegant horses and tragic deer march by on the walls in a timeless round. We can only guess their sense, but the emotion these works powerfully arouse in us leaves us with the overwhelming conviction that those people were as human as we are; or put it this way, we are as human as they were. *We recognize ourselves.* That moves us strongly. Unconsciously, it affects our appreciation, as the most essential trait of art: It is us! It's me! Other (conscious) meaning can only follow. In all other aspects we are different from our ancestors, and we don't know nor understand the meaning they gave to their lives. Their art, though, is still able to communicate; it communicates the unbroken chain of the human kind. That is an extraordinary message to modern global man; to each of us individually.

MAJOR WORKS AND MONUMENTS

Argentina, Cuevas de las Manos, painted stenciled hands
Austria, Vienna, Naturhistorisches Museum, sculpture *Venus of Willendorf*
Australia, Nawarla Gabarnmang, rock paintings, *kangaroos, birds, snakes*
Czech Republic, Brno, Moravian Museum, sculpture *Venus of Dolni Vestonice*

France, Montignac, Lascaux cave, wall and ceiling paintings, *bulls, horses, deer*
France, Pont-d'Arc, Chauvet cave, wall and ceiling paintings, *bulls, hyenas, panthers, bears*
France, Sarlat, Cro-Magnon, carvings, tools
Germany, Tübingen, Universitätsmuseum, sculpture, *Venus of Hohle Fels*

Russia, Kapova cave, wall and ceiling paintings, *mammoths, rhinos, horses*
South Africa, San Bushmen, rock paintings, *lions, cows, giraffes, tapirs*

South Africa, Blombos cave, *ochre preparing kits*
Spain, Altamira cave, wall paintings, *bulls, cows*
Spain, Nerva cave, wall and ceiling paintings, *seals*

3. **Art and Magic**

From the *natural* point of view (e.g., anatomy, physiology, biology, DNA) the species *Homo Sapiens Sapiens* has not changed since the Paleolithic era. With us change is social, *cultural*. What is more, change is one of our most typical traits, taking place beyond our will, or wish. And, it seems in our time, in accelerating speed.

With words and images as signs and symbols, which have existence not depending on the object they stand for, man could communicate with beings that were not there. Animals communicate with voice and limbs, in direct contact, *here and now*. Speech is different in that it can reach the present person *and* the absent; a (human) word can be repeated by another human without losing its precise meaning. A visual sign has sense independent on the time or space of its making or its maker. It has its own existence. So for humans the "no-man's land" is not empty but loaded with immanent presence. The air is not just fresh, it is inhabited by all that is ever said and seen. Words and images stay in the mind where they give birth to a virtual reality. Man is never alone; invisible spirits, good and bad, are watching over him night and day. That was (and is) the human condition, the condition for civilization. Spirits built the human society by producing a permanent oscillation between hope and fear, conflict and harmony, joy and terror, knowledge and doubt, life and death. Spirits, being invisible, were the domain of art. This *spiritual* fact, or magic, was universal and dominated human communities from very early on, so as to make art, including dance and music, their almost sole industry, blending in all else. Magic never disappeared from any civilization, though its importance and impact would diminish. Modern official culture has often neglected it, ignored, marginalized or combated; without lasting success. In their purest and strongest forms ancestral magic survived into our time in the art of nations living in the equatorial regions of Africa, Australia, Polynesia and Amazonia, all in danger of extinction.

The *mask* is the universal and most typical art product in this field, lending its limitless expressions and craft to a striking concept of the nature of spiritual communication. This concept turns ordinary reality inside out: not you observe the mask but the mask observes you, and indeed penetrates you with all its spiritual power, taking possession of you beyond the reality of your body and mind. In fact, reality belongs to the artifact, not to the woman or the man who projects it or is subjected to it. Reality is exclusively spiritual, and the mask represents it and makes it visible in fascinating, often terrifying, (rarely pretty) forms, all symbolic and overruling the laws of the physical world. Closely related to the mask is the practice of scarifications, mutilations and tattoos, always trying to transform and submit the body to the invisible world of the spirit.

Magic as a world view was the price the human animal paid for its grown brain and enhanced social capacities. It was also the prize that gained it its notions of consciousness and spiritual essence. It would strengthen the sense of community and guide the human story toward what we call the Neolithic revolution, a technological acceleration that started to take place around 12,000 years ago, in the Near East and Mediterranean lands. Agriculture, baked pottery and domestic animals were among the extraordinary novelties of these times. A certain division of labor and the living together of several families in villages and soon in towns were the design of this epoch for the rest of history. Hierarchy of wealth and power, warfare and religion came into their own, the roots of which, like the magic, went down into Paleolithic times and beyond. Art was the means of participation in the rites of life, such as the society prescribed them and a privileged cast of men imposed them.

Art changed within these new societies. However little we can understand from archeological deductions, virtually all known artworks are interpreted as being in the service of religion. Now this is certainly exact, if we acknowledge in the term religion the overwhelming part of magic, and we are aware of an essential difference with modern societies. We consider religion an isolated cultural activity standing on its own, like sports, or cooking, submitted to individual choice. Not so in the older world views, traces of which continue to exist today (*"In God We Trust"* is the official motto of the US since... 1956). There the human business and the supernatural were inseparable, intricately interwoven. Super nature dominated nature. Politics and sexuality, medicine and agriculture, war and peace, marriage and travel—every step in life, however ordinary, was also a step in another reality, the essential one, transcending the senses. Art and magic were still virtually synonymous, impossible to separate. The role of art was to reach out to the higher essences, to bring this mystic world under our eyes, into our hands. Art stood on the bridge between nature and super nature; it established the bond of the one with all, merging the individual in the whole. The visual arts didn't stand alone; they were one with architecture, theatre, dance, music and poetry and together they sought unison with nature. In their subtle and grandiose interplay they opened the human experience to the notion of sacredness. Here the individual could merge with the cosmos, or the god.

Neolithic art conquers the human figure (female more than male) in a surprising array of formal diversity, always stylized. Animals are ubiquitous, realistic or poetic; they are still an embodiment of the spirit, gods in all mythologies. Art objects represent (or rather present) the spiritual dimension of every human fact and act, from birth to grave. Never see them as just "pleasant" imitations of nature, or designs for the sake of design, made "for fun". No, aesthetics is a marginal concern and there is no fun whatsoever. These pieces are *inspired* per definition, they carry a *spirit* from above or below, and that is why they display dignity in form at any scale.

Many small pieces might have had *private* use, as amulets or sacrifices or family protectors. Monumental art seems rarified in comparison to the functional crafts, pottery, jewelry and weapons. In reality, an important part of the *public* works was of great formal discretion or austerity, human intervention being minimal: standing stones, poles, trees or trunks, even mountains, water pieces, or clearances in the forest. Here we see how the "creator" of art is the public that venerates it. Natural accident or "mother earth" had formatted the magic mind. It would take long before the religions accessed to precise forms for their pantheons and would abandon the mysteries. Now man was still a natural accident himself, and his art was a pact with the living earth and even with the heavens. Religions never abandoned the axiom of the sacred and the arts never ceased to be their language and form. Into our very days, now the sports and politics have taken the place of mass religion in the West, denying spiritual essence, music and art, poetry and architecture are the means to produce overwhelming effects on the individual mind.

Whoever visited Stonehenge will not forget the majesty of the ruined temple, the grandeur of the pillars on the hill, the marvel of the site, captivating the movements of the sun and the stars, a project the ambitious builders in Neolithic Britain were ready to affront with sensitivity, skill, and sacrifice. The impact, on us too, is sacred and we are tempted to search for "inspiration" from a more than human genius for the good of the people.

Modern society as a whole refutes the magic. Have we, moderns, lost this notion or need of constant relation with the invisible, beyond the limits of time and place? Not so sure! Our bodies are of the Cro-Magnon make. Since fifty millennia at least they function according to that vintage model and we find it back in our reflexes of fear, anger, joy and even speech.

Showing a photo to a friend you say "that's Grandma." You don't say, "That is a flat diminutive black and white image of the now deceased woman who was my Grandma." No, it *is* Grandma, and the more so since she's dead. We run around with pictures of our loved ones, and we look at them as utterly real, smiling when they smile, lying when they lie, crying when they cry. Pictures and cell phones are in part our amulets and talismans. We can't resist to their call. They soothe our anguish and they have us suffer for it. They are our connection to the unseen. On a more solemn level we are awe struck by the images of discoveries science made since Darwin and Einstein in the cosmos and the evolution of life on earth. They renewed our notion of the sacred in nature.

Religions steadily lose their grip on our spiritual ambitions, but art often still plays its Neolithic role: connecting us to the absent and to the spirit, whatever we think that may be. Museums are temples; artworks idols and relics; our trips to them pilgrimages. More important is this reflection: Artists search, many of them unconsciously, but without shame, after this *"inspiration from a more than human genius"* for the good of the human kind; and only in art (poetry, music, theatre) this inspiration is sometimes retrieved and made visible. Maybe the quest for the sacred is indeed the deepest human trait.

MAJOR WORKS AND MONUMENTS

Australia, Sydney, Australian Museum, Masks from Melanesia

Chad, Ennedi, *Beautiful Ladies*

France, Carnac, fields of menhirs

France, Corsica, standing megaliths, *Armed Men*

France, Paris, Musée des Arts Premiers (Museum of Primordial Arts), Masks, totems, etc.

Great Britain, London, British Museum, Masks

Great Britain, Stonehenge, megalithic temple

Greece, Cycladic figurines

Japan, Aomori (Honshu), *Sannai Maruyama,* town of the Jômon civilization

Malta, Valletta, National Museum of Archeology, *Sleeping Lady*

Niger, Dabous, *Giraffes*

Palestinian Territory, Jericho, West Bank city excavations,

South Africa, Cape Town, South Africa Museum, *Coldstream Burial Stone*

Switzerland, Zug, Africa Museum

USA, Philadelphia, PA, Penn Museum, Collection of African Art, Masks

4. **Art and Death**

The art we know from Paleolithic and Neolithic times has often been discovered in burial places. Humans would bury their dead, bones or ashes, not abandon them. Humans were the first living beings to know that they would surely die: no other knowledge has triggered consciousness more efficiently. Time was born when humans died.

There was being and not being. How to bridge the two?

Death was the great mystery. That speaking creature became mute like a painting, and its moving body became rigid like a statue. The corpse was covered with prayers and songs (to chase the silence?): all the moving rituals and stories that have generated religion. If there were the means, the corpse was offered also all that the living could have wished, food and clothes and jewelry, weapons and gold . . . and *life itself* (or its secret). Here the river of art found its bed.

How lifelike, how *alive!* we say, as the highest praise for art. Let us be aware why we repeat such common places. Deep in our memory art engraves the sign of our mortality, reminding us of the frightening unity of life and death.

Without death, no art.

Immobility and silence are art's identity and grandeur.

To our remote ancestors art suspended death; it became the vehicle to another life, a higher life.

No people have cultivated death more than the Egyptians, they were very artistic indeed. The vastest monuments ever conceived by man are the Pyramids; they are supposed to be graves. According to the Egyptian language the *image* is the *life*; we would say the soul, or true reality. Art (not the artist though) created life. (This is what the Hebrews denied, stating that God had created life and created man after his *image;* they therefore called all other images idolatry). The kings (*Pharaohs*) and queens and their ministers would have their *lifelike* statues of overpowering size hewn in hard rock or with convincing truth in precious stone and metals. Only relatively few have survived: they would typically be destroyed by rival dynasties having usurped their power; they would erase them not just for reasons of propaganda, but to conquer their real life.

The ultimate artwork, one might say, was for the Egyptians the human body itself after death, when the soul started a voyage to new life, as described in the verses of the Book of the Dead. The more a culture believed in a purely spiritual afterlife, the more we see its attachment to the earthly vessel of it.

The corpse was embalmed with infinite care and laid in a wooden coffin, itself conceived as a rigid body with a face mask, which was painted or sculpted inside and outside with a multitude of images, some utterly realistic, others a most simple sketch. This was possibly handed over to a sarcophagus in hard stone, decorated too. These images were believed to possess life and be as real as the food and drinks and cloth that were buried with the deceased. Art was in the service of death, alive in splendid tombs, the blessed witness and creator of afterlife. Countless beauties (scarabs, fish, cats, cows, hippopotamuses, birds, whatever one could see move between the Nile and the desert) made with extraordinary skill in all dimensions and all available materials (precious and semi-precious stones, noble woods and metals, fabrics, ceramics and paint) were buried with the dead, sealed in the tomb, and never to be seen again by human eyes. Unless robbers and archeologists broke the charm and entered into those artistic afterworlds.

Art victorious over time and fate: for thousands of years art had no deeper sense. Death frightens us. To counter its menace we produce offspring, physically. Spiritually, we make images with dead matter that will *live* beyond our time. Death stands hidden at the very origin of our creativity, joining the quest for the sacred as one of its deepest reasons.

The Pyramids of the plateau of Giza on the west bank of the Nile are not only gigantic; they are wonders of architectural skill. The mystery of their coming into existence and their meaning is as great as their size. How mysterious it is then that many centuries later, in a region that had with Egypt no known connections, Mexico and Middle America, a new wave of Pyramid building took place, equally majestic, equally skillful, equally raising the question of how and why. Here as in Egypt, the problems of the dating of the buildings, the identity of the builders and the iconographical messages are regularly reexamined.

At the very end of its independency, around the beginning of the Christian (or common) era, while its civilization was absorbed by the Roman Empire, Egypt offered, as a last flame of its culture to the dead, an original contribution to the changing world: the so called Fayum mummy portraits. Painted on cloth or on wood, they are the most penetrating effigies imaginable of usually unknown human faces. They appear to us so poignantly natural, that the distance between life and death (or between millenniums) seems to magically disappear for a moment.

Christianity imposed on Western cultures a very different approach of the reality of death: it was proof of the evil nature of life on earth. In its art a unique vision of Christ, venerated as Godhead and Savior, would present him as dead, attached to a cross, the instrument of his cruel execution by Roman authority. For fifteen hundred years this *Crucifix* would become the most widespread image and symbol of a vital and conquering civilization. Death as the terrestrial condition for a future resurrection would occupy the center of its artistic energy and reflection.

MAJOR WORKS AND MONUMENTS

China, Xinjiang, Qawrighul (Chinese: Gumugou), *white mummies*

Egypt, Abu Simbel, *temples of Ramses II and Nefertari*

Egypt, Deir el-Bahari, *temple of Hatshepsut*

Egypt, Cairo, Museum of Egyptian Antiquities, *Tomb of Tutankhamen*

Egypt, Cairo, Giza Plateau, *Pyramids of Cheops (or Khufu), Kephren (or Khafre) and Mykerinos*

Egypt, Cairo, Giza Plateau, *Sphinx*

Egypt, Cairo, Museum of Egyptian Antiquities, *Fayum mummy portraits*

Egypt, Luxor, Karnak, Valleys of the Kings and Queens, *temples, obelisks*

Egypt, Saqqara, *Djoser Pyramid*

Germany, Berlin, Egyptisches Museum, Tell El-Amarna excavations, *Akhenaton and Nefertiti busts*

Great Britain, Greenwich, Collection Steven A. Cohen, Damien Hirst, *The Physical Impossibility of Death in the Mind of Somebody Living*

Great Britain, London, British Museum, *Rosetta stone*

Guatemala, Tikal, *Mayan Pyramids*

Mapplethorpe, Robert, *Self-Portrait with Skull* (silver gelatin print)

Mexico, La Venta, *Giant Olmec Head*

Mexico, Teotihuacan Pyramids

Mexico, Yucatan Pyramids

Peru, Caral, *Pyramids and Amphitheater*

USA, New York, Metropolitan Museum of Art, *Temple of Dendur*

5. **Art, Space, and Time**

From these early times on, art presents a contradiction. It serves the ideal, the spirit, the beyond and the timeless, in pieces of work that are most earth bound, place determined, and time restricted. Archeologists date cultures with great precision analyzing their *crafts:* pottery, stone, bronze and iron tools and weapons, objects of daily use. They situate the *arts* back to their precise regions: statues, relief sculptures, murals in paint or in more resistant glazed bricks, objects in gold, silver, crystal, and glass. We "elevate" them to be "art" as they are related to government, religion, justice and war, in other words the great human affairs. Between art and craft the distinction is far from absolute.

Here continues the contradiction: the higher the art, the greater our need to designate the narrowest (geographic) space it responds to, representing one territory, one people, one city, one clan, one ruler, one god. And again: the greater art, the stronger our desire to make precise its age, its century, its year. In fact, art celebrates the exact meeting of the co-ordinates of time and space. Its form will be called style. History is the collection of those meeting points.

Let me try to put this also more simply, so you will appreciate the paradox. You have heard people say that great art is timeless. Now you understand that art is; but it is also typically not. Art is a (or *the*) marker of time past. It teaches us the physical reality of time. But at the same time art teaches us the spiritual reality of time and space. It always invites us to join another epoch, as well as another place on the earth. Art is the call from far. Our spirit answers to the call of past time and spaces, petrified in an artwork. In so doing art liberates us from our own age; we can be timeless and space free. We need this from time to time, like we need air and light: we need to join our ancestors. Through their art they will speak us about our world.

History is the *written* story of mankind. In the fourth millennium BCE between the Euphrates and the Tigris, script was invented, a joint venture merging speech and image into signs in the service of rapid and verifiable communication. It became soon the backbone of complex societies all over the globe: Sumer and Egypt and Greece, China and India, Inca, Mayan and Aztec empires. In the process history was separated (distilled) from mystery. Art's specific role became more narrow and more clear, visualizing the invisible part that humans have always seen in the visible. The geography and history of the arts were born, punctuated by ever varying styles. As such art was called to be the privileged and eloquent witness of the long march of human civilization.

The concrete result for you of these abstract considerations is to realize how we, spectators of the arts, we always and almost obsessively relate an art work to its origin, geographic and historic. We admire its fatherland for having produced it and we presume strongly that the arts and the land have mutually fertilized each other, that the arts between them resemble each other as family members. We feel that we can understand the one through the other, like a language or a dialect. Countries without "their" art do not exist in the face of the world and an art piece with no birthplace is beyond our imagination, while the slightest artefact (a coin or a clay tablet) gets the status of art if only it is a rare enough document of its time or place. In museums labels link artists systematically to their homeland and their age; and an artist's nationality is presented as his or her honor, or in times of conflict despised as his or her fault. Cities are mentioned as their place of birth or death and it puts them on the map for pilgrims or tourists. The most famous artists are venerated by their compatriots as national heroes, in school books, as statues, stamps and street names, like generals and scientists, and more than the latter they are described with musicians and poets as the typical representation of their century and their nation. The "universal" and "timeless" products of the human genius must teach us a humble truth: that we belong like wine to our vintage and our soil. Indeed, we don't need to be art experts to distinguish an Assyrian king from an Egyptian Pharaoh, or a Buddha from a Madonna, or (the statues of) George Washington from Booker T. Washington. The arts oblige us to recognize both the infinite variety of civilizations and our capacity to appreciate them and often to admire them.

MAJOR WORKS AND MONUMENTS

France, Paris, Musée du Louvre, Stele of Hammurabi
France, Paris, Musée du Louvre, glazed brick friezes from Darius the Great's palace, Susa
Germany, Berlin, Pergamonmuseum, Ishtar Gates
Great Britain, London, British Museum, the Cyrus Cylinder
Great Britain, London, British Museum, Assyrian relief sculptures, *the Siege of Lachish*
Great Britain, London, British Museum, Akkadian cuneiform tablet script of Gilgamesh epic
Iran, Persepolis, the Apadana of Darius and Xerxes
Iraq, ruins of Babylon, Nimrod, Nineveh
Iraq, Bagdad, National Museum, Sumerian cuneiform tablets
Iraq, Bagdad, National Museum, statue of Entemena of Lagash
Iraq, Bagdad, National Museum, Warka Vase
Iraq, Ur, Ziggurat Nanna

6. **Art and Order**

Toward the end of the Neolithic era, happening by the way in very different moments in the diverse regions of the world (in some cases never happening at all), coinciding with the beginning of historic time, complex societies, as opposed to families and tribes, had become the dominant form of human cohabitation. We usually see a city surrounded by land and villages, soon groups of cities and the land and villages in between. Some names of cities, still alive as ruins, entered into history, others into legend: like Babylon, Troy, Knossos, Machu Picchu, Avalon. Developing the distribution of food and security, cities imposed ever-growing measures of order to the citizens, concerning all systems of human interaction and rules of power and influence. We discover all over the globe innumerable (and similar) efforts of societies building roads, issuing laws and coins; add to this the regulation of transportation, on land and sea, imposition of taxes and warfare, stabilization of regional languages and alphabets, politics, and religions. The history of Greece is in this context of particular importance for the Western world, until today. The way social action was organized in a Greek city has been (with the essential exception of slavery and gender relationships) the most inspirational model for the greatest numbers of modern societies. The interrelation between the arts, sciences, politics, and morals strikes us as familiar, and even admirable.

The Greeks developed the idea that the universe should be a *cosmos*, which means order. It was the great system of relationships defying the menace of a primordial *chaos*. Harmony in all realms (even that of the gods) depended on it. The human society in all its parts should be the reflection of the cosmic principles. These principles, the great logic keeping all things together, became object of study and research. Here stands the beginning of philosophy and science. The arts, with temple architecture as their leading force, express this research in symbolic form, and all art forms can be seen as symbolic of this research.

The Greek temple is a large house surrounded on three or four sides by a row of columns that support the roof. Nothing is simpler than that. But all the elements conform to precise and fundamental relationships. Grandeur and beauty depend on these, more than on sheer size or material. The temples of all the gods in all the cities and islands resemble each other like so many variations on a single theme, and the theme is order as it can be expressed by interrelationship of the parts. The white marble *fluted* columns in particular, which was practically all one would see of the temple architecture, represent the governing principles of this order, and that is how we name them and distinguish between them: orders. Their measurements, both as the group and individually, are defined by specific proportions of mathematic simplicity, creating harmony to the eye and to the mind. Originally, there were only three *orders*. The one considered most noble between them was the austere Doric order, without a base. The more elegant and light one was called Ionic, with a flat upper part in spiral volute form, the capital. The somewhat later Corinthian order, highest and most imposing, had rich vegetal decoration added to the volutes in the well-developed capital.

Since the Greeks we realize how art stands for the creation and maintenance of a symbolic order in a threatening natural disorder. The terms of this order, which visually express fundamental values, experienced as beauty, differ from society to society, though they pretend to be based on rules of universal harmony. For the Ancient Greeks the rules were numeric: mathematics as we know it, was a Greek invention. Numbers were supposed, by their relationships (or proportions), to govern the reality of value: in geometry and astronomy, music and the visual arts, education, politics and the art of war. With the help of numbers they related all to all. Proportions offered clarity into the darkest problem. The most mysterious proportion escapes from final definition; it is called *divine* or the *golden mean,* $(a+b)/a = a/b$, valued as $1.6180...$, represented by the letter *phi,* Φ, after the Greek sculptor Phidias. The beauty of the Parthenon, we are told, depends on its application into the smallest detail. The other mysterious number was pi, π, $3.1416....$, establishing the relation between the diameter and the perimeter of a circle. The first description of the values Φ and π was Greek; they were, however, found as a constructive principle as early as the Pyramids of Egypt, as well as in nature itself. They were certainly amongst the secrets of the builders of the Pre-Columbian pyramids in Central America, as well as of the Christian cathedrals in the European Middle Ages. Φ made a remarkable come-back in modern times, in epoch-making buildings by architects like Frank Lloyd Wright and Le Corbusier.

The Greek building system with its columns of various orders has been one of the most successful in history, ancient and modern. The Romans took it over during half a millenary, and one millenary later the Renaissance, Baroque and Neoclassical art movements reintroduced it with many variations in Europe. It marks the styles of Saint Peter's Basilica in Rome, of the royal Louvre palace in Paris and the British Museum in London. From there it entered as the architectural style of prestigious buildings into the American, Asian and North-African colonies of Spain, Britain and France.

The United States kept a strong nostalgia for columns; the Neo-classical style, inspired by the purest Greek examples, reigned in architecture in the days of the War of Independence and was never betrayed. Especially the Southern states continue to erect columns with obstinacy and almost superstition for unquestioned formal symbolism. Not much attention is given, though, to their original laws of proportion and even less to their material. Such is our relation to other famously invoked Greek institutions, like democracy, sports or sexuality, often equally whimsical.

In modern history, beginning around 1850, the idea of order in art is more ambivalent than it was before. The cause lays in a society where the unstoppable rise of technology is deployed to increase the control of its citizens. In recent times this order is converging with performing new means of communication, like the Internet, Google, Facebook, smart phones and so on. Invented in the name of freedom, they penetrate into our private existence, predetermine our actions and deliver us to ideas and entities beyond our knowledge or control. Order, in older civilizations a protection against blind social and natural violence, becomes itself a form of blind violence. Since more than a hundred years now, art makes us aware of the danger of these life-size contradictions. It reacts to these invisible powers with the violence of symbolic destruction, laying bare the mechanisms of the threats. The formal results yield typically to screaming disorder and deconstruction. They cause screaming anger and refusal with the public. However, modern artists too, from the chaos they bring about, immediately start to build the visible signs of a new order, personal, exemplary, miniscule, hopeful. With time the public accepts them, appropriates them. The underlying message is clear: a better world can only be born out of the destruction of the existing order. Of course, this process happens within the symbolic and very orderly walls of the contemporary art museums.

MAJOR WORKS AND MONUMENTS

Greece, Athens, the Acropolis, temple of Athena-Parthenos (Parthenon)

Greece, Athens, the Acropolis, Erechteion

Greece, Athens, the Agora, temple of Apollo Patroos

Greece, Attica, Aegina, temple of Aphaea

Greece, Delphi, temple of Apollo, Oracle

Greece, Epidaurus, temple of Asclepius, the theatre

Greece, Olympia, temple of Zeus

Italy, Paestum, temples of Hera, Poseidon, Demeter

Italy, Sicily, Agrigento, temples of Concordia, Juno

Italy, Sicily, Segesta, Doric temple

Italy, Sicily, Selinunte, temple of Hera

Libya, Cyrene, temples of Zeus, Apollo

McCarthy, Paul, *Piccadilly Circus*, video

Turkey, Assos, temple of Athena

Turkey, Didyma-Miletus, temple of Apollo

Turkey, Priene, temple of Athena Polias

Turkey, Sardis, temple of Artemis

7. **Art and the Human Body**

Greek civilization developed a strong idea into a fundamental artistic law: that the ultimate goal of art is the representation of the human body. With this claim art might be said to have closed a full cycle since its Paleolithic beginnings. In philosophy, Greek thought is often resumed in the phrase: Man is the measure of all things. Take it quite literally: the measure of the human body, its form and its mind, is the origin and aim of knowledge and insight. This assesses a great deal of Greek religious imagination. The gods are seen as humans who will not fail, so the Greeks represent them, in thought and in marble, as flawless bodies: free standing, nude, confident, universal. This body is the shortest formula of perfection. Dynamic and relaxed, young but mature, rooted in visible reality, but reaching out into the ideal, in noble stone or metal, the Greeks have offered the world the ideal of the body and the body as an ideal.

In the first half of the first millennium BCE, in the wake of new directions in spirituality, new attitudes towards art came to the fore in the Mediterranean area. They took distance from the animistic, polytheistic and essentially magic world view, still omnipresent, but now condemned as superstitious. They epitomized two new metaphysical standpoints, which would leave their stamp on art for centuries to come. Both are born from a changing notion concerning the human body, one negative, the other positive. The monotheistic Israelites banned, by divine law, every kind of effigy of the human figure, strictly respected as the image of its jealous creator. Representations of living creatures were shunned as idolatry. By consequence the arts concentrated on decorative functions. The Greeks, on the contrary, exalted the human figure, for them equally the form of their gods. The visual arts were here elevated to the study of the principles of the good, the true and the beautiful, laid down in the nude body, representing *par excellence* divine presence in the visible world. Art could become an autonomous spiritual exercise.

The body referred to now had nothing fortuitous. The human figure (male first, going by the name of a god, Apollo, Zeus, or called *kouros* in art history, meaning *young man*, often a victorious athlete from the Olympic games; joined later by the female, principally the goddess Aphrodite, or Nymphs or an anonymous young woman called *koure* or *kore* in art history) at its divine best was conceived in Greece as obeying to a complete set of proportions, or revealing them. This same set, when applied to the sports, would make him the best athlete in the games; to war the best fighter in the battle; to music the best singer in the theatre; in art the truest to the eye. The study of proportions imposed body forms that were beyond individual taste, but set the artist free from sterilizing repetition as was so often the case in neighboring regions like Egypt. The body could assume various positions and still be perfect from all angles. The challenge was to establish the form in which nature came closest to the idea. This introduced in the minds the sense of artistic competition between the past and the presence, where the prize was immortality of the artist's name. In less than two centuries the marble body liberated itself from a rigid frontal block of stone to become a young man or woman of admirable natural dignity. This path of liberating progression has proven of colossal influence on the West, but also on the East, where the Indian and even Chinese traditions have sometimes succumbed to their charms. The Greek gods are gone, but the statues stay. We still call them with their divine names: Zeus (Jupiter), Hermes (Mercury), Athena (Minerva) or Artemis (Diana) and above all Aphrodite (Venus) and Apollo. However we must add that the Greek originals are rare, we know them from their Roman copies. In celebrated Greek painting we have only famous names left, like Zeuxis, who painted grapes so well, it deceived the birds; or Parrhasios, whose illusionist curtains deceived even the eye of Zeuxis. Their works have never been discovered. We are lucky we can follow their exciting development thanks to the excellent pottery painters with their red or black figures.

An elaborate and apparently definitive system of proportions was codified in a little booklet by the sculptor Polycleitus in the fifth century BCE under the name of the *Canon*. He demonstrated his theory in his famous *Doryphoros, (the Spear Bearer)*. Every part (of the body) must be related to the whole according to relatively simple numerical ratios. Ideas like *symmetry, rhythm, equilibrium* and *commensurate* enter into the artist's vocabulary. The most important formal principle is called (in Italian) *contrapposto*. Here every proposition is balanced by a subtle counter-proposition. For instance, if one leg carries the weight, the other moves freely; if one shoulder recedes, the other advances; if the torso turns right, the head turns left, and so on, without exception for any part. The total of these interrelationships creates the necessary equilibrium for the object to stand and for the eye to be pleased.

The *Canon* marks the classical moment in ancient art, of which the greatest artist was Phidias, the sculptor of the Parthenon pediments and friezes; in the same temple he made the statue of Athena as well as that of Zeus in Olympia, each in ivory and gold, close to 40 feet high (both lost). The *Canon* was a code, never a law. It was the first statement about art by art itself, where the form equals the content in importance. It might even surpass it, the form having become itself expression of thought (and not of *a* thought). This was fertile enough to serve as the point of departure for Hellenistic, Roman, and later Renaissance, Baroque, and Neoclassical sculpture and painting. We remark that its leading principle was not to copy reality but to surpass it by study and selection of the best, and transform it to the ideal. In so doing the Greeks anchored art and beauty in the revolutionary thought systems of their time; they kept authority till the end of the 19th century.

They didn't disappear even then. Every day we see around us how the Greek vision of corporeal beauty has formed our taste and is still powerfully with us: not in the arts of painting and sculpture, though, but in advertisement, fashion, photography and film. It even tempts irresistibly the societies of Asia and Africa.

MAJOR WORKS AND MONUMENTS

Germany, Munich, Glyptothek, *Munich Kouros*
Germany, Munich, Glyptothek, pediment sculptures of the temple of Aphaea, Aegina
Great Britain, London, British Museum, pediment sculptures from the Parthenon
Greece, Athens, Archeological Museum of Piraeus, *Piraeus Apollo*
Greece, Athens, National Museum of Archeology, *Kritian Boy*

Greece, Athens, National Museum of Archeology, *Kroisos Kouros,*
Greece, Athens, National Museum of Archeology, *Peplos Kore*
Greece, Athens, National Museum of Archeology, pediment sculptures from the temple of Zeus, Olympia
Greece, Athens, National Museum of Archeology, *Zeus* or *Poseidon of Artemision*

Greece, Delphi, Delphi Museum, *Charioteer*

Italy, Agrigento, Museo Archeologico Nazionale, *Ephebe of Agrigento*

Italy, Rome, Vatican Museums, Myron of Eleutherae, *Diskobolos* (Roman replica)

Italy, Naples, Museo Archeologico Nazionale,

Polycleitus, *Doryphoros* (« Canon », Roman replica)

Italy, Reggio di Calabria, Palazzo Campanella, *Riace Warriors*

Netherlands, Leiden, Museum van Oudheden, Attic amphora, *Goddess Athena and goddess Nikè*

USA, New York, N.Y., Metropolitan Museum of Art, *Attica Kouros*

8. **Art and Power**

Art in all ages has been the attribute of power: political, religious, economic.

Power over *the other* is a natural need, inherent to the principle of life and evolution. It drives individuals and societies to dominate the rivals, to possess or eliminate them.

Art being an entity beyond use, it has special attraction for those who are beyond the necessity of earning their daily bread: the elite, the aristocracy or oligarchs, the rich and the powerful. They choose art to exalt their social position, trying to give it a function in the service of their social class. We associate art easily with leisure, luxury, luster, and limitless expenses, with rare materials, expert handwork, endless labor force, and certainly with excesses of size and costs. We like to dwell in the fantasy of an apparently beautiful lifestyle we ascribe to the happy few; art seems to be the signpost of their sometimes extravagant privileges. We forget that our eye is not fixed then upon the deeper layers of art; rather on something like its gilt frame. In our time it is generally not art we encounter there, but crafts like fashion, cuisine, jewelry and cinema, things that pass.

However, the link between arts and politics can be described as a mutual fascination since the deepest past. Power needs the arts, and the arts need the powerful. The power in place has always and everywhere used the arts to justify and magnify its legitimacy, and thus to enhance its psychological grip on the subjects. Without it the history of the arts would not have had its major importance in all civilizations. It is for us sometimes morally difficult to acknowledge that great art has been produced in the service of principles we reject. Palaces of emperors and kings may fill us with pity for the population. Let us then not forget that the greatest palace was inexpensive in comparison with the smallest war. The monuments we now include in art history were often the constructions of peace. They served as means of government, symbols of political unity and national identity, promotion of ideological principles such as religion and law, security and public pride, redistribution of riches, employment of the workers and of non-verbal communication with the people. Hopefully they would impress the neighbor, a potential enemy of course, and keep him astray. Or persuade him to compete in splendor.

Look at it also in this way: while the powerful consider the arts quite shamelessly as their due, the arts have often had a sort of revenge, taking over control and urging the powerful to go beyond all limits to obtain them. Art has an addictive influence on crowns, thrones, and capital. Many of the greatest achievements of human creativity were once the greatest temptation of their patrons and finally a cause of their fall. Art seems to be the ultimate territory to conquer. Or the ultimate reason for all other conquests. Even our billionaires build collections of art, paying for it billions rather than millions. Why? Is it its immortality or eternal youth, beauty, talent, or near divinity? These are the fundamental desires that art lays bare in the human heart, of which it is in fact the reason for being. Great inhumanity is often their price, paid for by the people. The legends of antiquity tell us this story: the great Pyramids and the Pharaohs, the hanging gardens of Babylon and Nebuchadnezzar, the temple of Jerusalem and King Solomon, the Parthenon and the Athenian Pericles. And even more mysterious is the unknown story of the giant Moai statues of Easter Island. Artistic ambitions finally caused their fall. True stories of pride and punishment. But the monuments stayed.

No story is more eloquent than the one of Cheng, king of Qin, the first Emperor of China, known as Shi Huangdi. The founding of the most powerful state of the world, China, still existing, the unification of its weights and measures, laws and writing system, completion of the Great(est) Wall, the construction of thousands of miles of roads, these deeds are almost eclipsed, or put in a new light by the recent discovery of his tomb, the most compelling artistic installation ever. In an artificial mountain, a petrified army of ten thousand more than life-size warriors guarded the jaded body of the merciless conqueror in his ultimate quest for everlasting life. And with success! While the son of the emperor was soon overthrown by furious peasants, and a new dynasty came to power, the terra cotta soldiers protected their feared genial master over two millennia long. They came to the light in 1974, to the astonishment of the historians and the public, a year or two before the death of the emperor's heir in the twentieth century, Chairman Mao Zedong. And here we see a moving example of what I called the revenge of art over brutal ambition and power: the spiritual aspirations and speculations of the proud emperor mean little more to us than ancient and cruel anecdote, but the inspired works of his numberless anonymous artists and artisans baffle us with admiration. Now not the emperor, but *the art* resuscitates, in all the glory of its emotional craft, setting an army of artists in the spotlights of the whole modern world. Mysterious power of art, which transforms the material defeat of the body of flesh and bone into a spiritual victory of the mind! Powerful art, we say rightfully.

In modern states political and religious powers have handed the arts over to specialized administrations, protecting the nation's monuments against decay and loss, promoting its museums, old and new, for the greatest benefit of the tourist industries. Indeed, for the benefit of modern humankind. In a certain measure the arts have become the political and diplomatic cement of reconciliation between former enemies; a growing force of peace, respect and insight in the creative differences between populations and civilizations; one of the rare aspects of modern life that gives authentic hope for the future. We must proclaim that a nation that protects and promotes its arts protects and promotes its culture, its economy, its environment, its justice, its children.

Power is not a prerogative of top politics or economics. Its seeds are in each of us, and in fact art reveals its intimate nature. It belongs to our time to underline this psychological side of the question: artistic talent is in itself a potential source of power and its sensation, constructive and personal in principle, is an alternative to ordinary social strive and competition. The modern living artist finds strong satisfaction in the act of a unique production, in the sensation of autonomy, in the pursuit of a personality standing up in a society that seriously threatens these values. We as the public are comforted by their radiant example and we can't help regard it as a virtuous model. The personal experience of power over someone's own life pays back in part for the lack of social influence or financial security experienced by many living artists today.

But artists are no angels. In their own universe, today more and more perverted by capitalism, the battle for influence and might can be as primitive and cruel as in the time of the last emperors. In the richest nations the art world is a true little state inside the state. It organizes itself indeed like the royal courts did in pre-modern times, with their privileges and nepotism, flows of public money and lack of public control, scandals and low morality, ennui and etiquette, disdain for the common people, and palaces like forbidden cities complete with ministers and grand-viziers, eunuchs and lackeys, ephebes and courtesans, who admire all day long the new clothes of the emperor.

MAJOR WORKS AND MONUMENTS

Chile, Polynesia, Easter Island, 887 Moai monumental statues

China, Changping, Beijing, Ming Dynasty Tombs

China, Dongcheng, Beijing, The Forbidden City (former imperial palace)

China, the Great Wall

China, Lintong district, Xi'an, Shaanxi, *The Terracotta Army*, mausoleum of Shi Huangdi

China, Mancheng district, Hebei, Han dynasty tombs of Prince Liu Sheng and his wife Dou Wan

China, Mawangdui, Changsha, Hunan, Han dynasty tombs

China, Shaanxi, Xiangyang, *Yangling Mausoleum* and *Museum*

China, Shanghai, Shanghai Tower J-Hotel (highest hotel in the world)

Croatia, Split, palace of the Roman emperor Diocletian

France, Versailles, Royal Palace and Gardens (palace of King Louis XIV)

Germany, Schwangau, Neuschwanstein (palace of King Ludwig II of Bavaria)

Japan, Osaho & Mesaho, Imperial Family tombs

Japan, Sakai, Osaka, tomb of emperor Nintoku

Kazakhstan, Astana, tomb of a Scythian prince

Panama, Panama City, Trump Ocean Club (luxury housing complex)

Russia, Moscow, Kremlin (palace complex of emperors and presidents)

South Korea, Gongju, Chungcheongnam-do, tomb of king Muryeong

Spain, Madrid, El Escorial (palacemonastery of King Philip II)

Turkey, Istanbul, Topkapi (former palace of the sultan)

USA, Grant Park, Chicago, Ill., Magdalena Abakanowicz, *Agora*

9. Art and Conquest

Sometimes it is the destiny of one human existence to change the course of history. Alexander the Great of Macedon illustrates this idea with frightening force. His unparalleled 10-year campaign against the Greek city states, and Persia, Egypt, Bactria, even India, would have been soon forgotten, though, if in its wake new forms of society had not immediately given sense to all this warfare. These forms were Greek in origin and design, now given a new dimension by its confrontation with the Near East. Many cultural phenomena, from philosophy and politics to mathematics and urbanism, including the art of war and religion, merged here to become an invincible force of conquest, by assimilation and acculturation, of territories with strong own traditions. The result was what we name Hellenism, stretching from the Indus to the Danube and from the Black Sea to the Red Sea in states governed by dynasties descending from generals of Alexander's army. The visual arts were an acute testimony, if not a spearhead of its persuasive efficiency.

Maybe the best comparison to this historical phenomenon in the modern world would be the irresistible whirlwind of American culture upsetting centuries-old traditions in Europe and Asia and fertilizing them for a new age. In both cases the arts of the conquering power represented the future with such evidence that they replaced in part the use of weaponry.

In those times and in that space, the arts, sculpture in particular, taking their point of departure from the *ideal* of the classical Greek style, and its unfailing concentration on the human body as vehicle of all expression, now conquered the *real*. Emotional, psychological, socially daring subject matter on one hand, and the overwhelming, theatrical and virtuoso scale and skill on the other, turned the arts into a major actor on the stage of political propaganda and cultural prestige. New born cities with Greek names, Alexandria, Antioch, with Greek institutions, built in Greek architectural styles, erected impressive monuments, some of which are still known as the wonders of the ancient world: the Colossus of Rhodes, the Mausoleum of Halicarnassus, the Light House of Alexandria, the Artemis Temple of Ephesus, all destroyed. But the imposing Zeus Altar from Pergamum, partly saved, is today the pride of Berlin.

The great city of this world was Alexandria, the capital of Egypt under the Ptolemaic kings. It was here that the wise and the learned, the scientists and the researchers of the epoch met each other in the famous schools. A library, with the name of *Musaeum* (!), unrivaled in its time for its collections, kept the original manuscripts of its famous men, like the *Elements of Geometry*, by Euclid; the first measurement of the earth and the oldest maps by Eratosthenes, later replaced by the more well-known ones by Ptolemy; the writings on physics by Archimedes. It was here, too, that according to legend seventy-two rabbis from Palestine translated the Torah in seventy-two days from Hebrew into Greek, the *Septuagint*. The Greek language was then the *lingua franca* of the Mediterranean area in many fields, from commerce to science, just like English in our time around the Atlantic Ocean.

In the field of the arts, the men who had the classical style evolve into new directions were Greek, contemporary to Alexander, and we know their names and biographies: Praxiteles, Lysippus, Apelles and many more. Praxiteles, sculpting the first female nude, the goddess of love Aphrodite, opened the way for sensuous and even erotic themes as art, or art as the lasting answer to human desire; Lysippus invited the spectator to walk around the sculpted figure, or art achieving the conquest of the third dimension. Art became the study of the human race in all its tragic or comical, heroic or humble, divine or terrestrial attitudes. Protogenes and Apelles achieved these goals in painting; only stories of them remain. One tells us how Alexander the king honored Apelles the painter with the gift of his own royal mistress (and not just as a model). The greatest of all generals sensed that the arts were like an avant-garde of his never failing army. Not accidentally, such was the intuition of the student of the first philosopher of reality, Aristotle, who understood the arts as an instrument of discovery of the truth.

MAJOR WORKS AND MONUMENTS

France, Paris, Musée du Louvre, Alexandros of Antioch, *Venus of Milo*

France, Paris, Musée du Louvre, *Nike of Samothrace*

Germany, Berlin, Pergamonmuseum, Altar to Zeus, *Battle of Gods and Titans*

Germany, Berlin, Pergamonmuseum, Market Gates of Miletus

Greece, Athens, National Museum of Archeology, *Horse Rider of Artemision*

Greece, Athens, National Museum of Archeology, *Ephebe of Antikythera*

Italy, Naples, Museo Nazionale di Archeologia, Lysippus, *Farnese Hercules* (Roman replica)

Italy, Naples, Museo Nazionale di Archeologia, Philoxenos of Eretria (?), *Alexander Mosaic* (*The Battle of Issus,* Roman replica)

Italy, Rome, Vatican Museums, Athanadoros *e.a.*, *Laocoon* (Roman replica)

Italy, Rome, Vatican Museums, Praxiteles, *Aphrodite of Knidos* (Roman replica)

Italy, Rome, Vatican Museums, Leochares, *Apollo Belvedere* (Roman replica)

Italy, Rome, Musei Capitolini, Epigonos, *Dying Gaul* (Roman replica)

USA, New York, NY, Metropolitan Museum of Art, *Sleeping Eros* (bronze Roman replica)

10. **Art and Technical Skill**

Our word *art* comes from the Latin *ars,* which translated the Greek word *techne,* both words meaning *skill, know-how,* eventually *craft.* Many people today continue to assimilate art with skills. They wonder (in front of an old cathedral) "How could they achieve this *with the tools of their time?*" or they ask (in front of a meticulous portrait) "How long did that take?!" Or they are scandalized when they see paint thrown on the canvas by the buckets: "My little nephew can do better." Legitimate questions and remarks, but only partly right.

We say craft when the element of skill dominates that of art, when the visible dominates the invisible, or the manual the conceptual. The dividing line is blurred and moving. Pottery used to be a craft in the West, an art in the Far East. Decoration is usually seen as a craft, as are all things useful. Furniture or armors or daggers or clocks or automobiles, jewelry or tattoos, however beautiful they may look, fall in this domain. Think of this: you may be a genius artist and unrecognized, but an unrecognized craftsman simply doesn't know his trade. Art, though, welcomes skills and many enter into the success of a work. We moderns think, however, that the decisive factor that makes an object *art* is beyond the craft. Not so the Romans.

Skill is the proper use of tools. It preceded the notion of art in the humanoid genes, by millions of years. The use of tools is not uniquely human, either. Our sense of art expresses our ambivalent relation with them. We love our machines but we love our poor hands more. In a philosophical way we could resume the situation this way: tools point from the present toward the future (*where do we go?*), whereas art defines our present in regard to the past (*where are we from?*). Arts assess our identity, tools our fears and hopes. Tools, therefore, are profoundly typical of our species. It is one of our dominating traits to lay our trust in them for our progression. Some believe that we only have to make them more perfect to become perfect ourselves . . . The Romans seem, amidst our ancestors, to have embodied that idea. Patiently and with an unfailing art of warfare, they built an empire around the Mediterranean Sea, prevailing over the strongest existing nations. They kept it together for seven centuries, thanks to their roads, laws, and armies—and to their building industry. *Concrete* and *brick* as building materials and the *arch* and the *dome* as devices of construction distinguish them above all. Solid, efficient, functional, resistant, imposing, imperial, these terms define their creative impulses. Engineers, rather than artists, represented the genius of a state of political stability and material well-being. Their technical abilities and resources oblige us to the greatest respect and enthusiasm. So much so that we often forget that these rational Romans were also the most superstitious of all peoples.

Hellenistic in urbanism and architecture, the Romans embellished their cities and homes with Greek sculpture, copies being made almost industrially. The painters also honored the Greek styles, and not slavishly. The houses in Pompeii (the rare ones we know) were beautifully decorated, as must have been the palaces in Rome and in the many cities founded in the provinces, like Arles and Lyon, France, or Tarragona and Toledo, Spain, or Caesarea and Tiberias in Palestine: the mosaic floors with scenes from everyday life, the walls with frescoed scenes from mythology and literature. Public space was richly embellished, too, with statues, temples, altars and decorated columns; and so were the roads, lined by mortuary monuments. The wealthy dead were buried in lavishly sculpted sarcophagi. Decorative arts like glass and cameo cutting were brought to perfection. But we don't (or very rarely) know the names of their makers, in spite of their extraordinary skills, and nowhere more than in portraiture. The artist's status was low. It is in architectural engineering where we find Rome's greatest *original* creative strength: roads, bridges, aqueducts, amphitheaters, baths, and basilicas. Some surpass all imagination, inspire awe and admiration, and join our purest sense of art. This is inevitably the case of the *Pantheon* and the *Coliseum* in Rome or the *Pont-du-Gard* in the south of France.

More than any other, the Roman Empire reveals itself as the (unconscious) model for the modern world. Its imperialism, militarism and global ambitions, its materialism, legalism, technical prowess and communicative systems (media) offer striking comparisons with today's Western civilization. In this context the growing impact of *technology* (the new *tools*) on the arts in our culture is worth reflection.

Skills of all kinds have fascinated artists through the ages, and artists have often been brilliant inventors of techniques to better serve the whole of society. Manual and intellectual skills are a fundamental part of art history. However, the arts used to absorb the crafts. Technique was the handmaiden of art. In our time we see the roles slowly inverting, reminding us of the time when Greek creativity became Roman industry. The *new engineering* or technology takes the leading role, both in scale and public attention. It absorbs the arts. Art becomes the handmaiden of technology.

MAJOR WORKS AND MONUMENTS

Austria, Vienna, Kunsthistorisches Museum, *Gemma Augustea Cameo*
Croatia, Pula, Amphitheatre
France, Arles, Crypto-porticos
France, Orange, Triumphal Arch
France, Paris, Musée du Louvre, portrait bust of the emperor Hadrian
France, Remoulins, *Pont-du-Gard*
Great Britain, London, British Museum, *Portland Vase*
Great Britain, Northern England, *Hadrian's Wall*
Italy, Pompeii, *Villa of the Mysteries*
Italy, Rome, *Coliseum*

Italy, Rome, Forum, *Basilica of Maxentius*
Italy, Rome, Forum, *Trajan's Column*
Italy, Rome, Musei Capitolini, *Colossus of Constantine*
Italy, Rome, Musei Capitolini, *Equestrian Statue of Marcus Aurelius*
Italy, Rome, Museo Nazionale Romano, *Ludovisi Battle Sarcophagus*
Italy, Rome, *Pantheon*
Italy, Rome, Vatican Museums, *Augustus of Prima Porta*
Spain, Segovia, Aqueduct

11. Art and Identity

One of the greatest benefits people have drawn from the arts is what we could name the *forms* of identity. Societies have taken great advantage of the unifying effects of visual recognition and repetition; think of the impact of a national flag on human behavior. Many see here a convenient definition for the concept of culture. A most striking example living under our eyes is given by the Islam.

Islam, an Arabic word meaning *Submission (to God)*, is the last ancient empire and it defines itself as a religion. Inheritor of the Jews and the (Byzantine) Christians, Islam occupies all the territories of the Greco-Roman world, with the exception of Western Europe. It expands far beyond it in Africa and Asia. Without the need or ambition of national, political, or even theological unification, the cohesion of the empire is the fact of a sacred language, extended visually and infinitely into art. All art is therefore virtually Islam, and Islam virtually only art. All that comes out of trained hands or mouth is a *prayer;* art is too; it transforms matter into spirit. If all creativity is art, there is no art (in our sense of the word); there is craftsmanship, tradition, cult, culture. There is no artist, only the *work*, behind which the individuality of the worker has disappeared. There is no public either, because the whole community is the public. Every member of it understands, participates, relates, and sacrifices his or her individuality to the *work*. This art unifies, repeating in an endless refrain one and the same theme in endless variations. Art unifies all the competing parts of the society, it is above the society; it doesn't take part in the social dialogue. It is omnipotent and helpless, venerated and neglected, omnipresent and ignored. It never questions, it confirms. It cannot evolve or develop, it repeats. It has no history or future, no beginning or end. However visually rich or luxurious, art is spiritually virtuous and simple: it changes humble matter into astonishing beauty, wool into carpets to pray, stone into mosques, clay into ceramic tiles quoting the Quran, trees into gardens, water into fountains. It is always decorative, though educative, overwhelming though subordinate to a greater goal, which is purely spiritual and as such beyond the visible. It makes the stand for universal and timeless truth in a quotidian chaos. It offers before the eyes the relationship of all brothers and sisters in the world, turning them visually into one humankind, one earth, rendering grace to one godhead. This cosmic pretension exceeds the life of the individual.

The representation of the human form is typically prescribed. The preferred form is the decorative abstract line of the arabesque lending itself to endless variations on the alphabet, the vehicle of the Holy Scripture. Every line is calligraphy, found in ceramics, glass, metal and leather work, carpets, banners and precious books, all ornamental crafts the Islam promotes and excels in. All this comes together in the grandiose complexes of popular gathering and worship that are the mosques, with their courtyards, cupolas and minarets. But autonomous paintings and sculptures are foreign to this art.

Every person, young and old, recognizes her- or himself as part of the community called Islam, visualized by the anonymous arts. All receive here an identity, exceeding the personal one, because shared with all: an anonymous identity exceeding earthly life.

Exemplified by their respective vision of the arts, Islam and the West assume two opposite attitudes to culture and identity. And their more fanatic avant-gardes are in war. As often, in the battle the extremes meet. One is allowed to inquire if the West in our times does not develop a cultural identity of the Islamic kind, replacing unifying theology by unifying media technology. In this light 9/11 must be seen as more than a violent act of blind terrorism, but as the deed of a culture in danger of identity loss. And the U.S. equally violent reaction might be seen as very much the same. We experience the clash of two art views, two world views. It is therefore important to mention the exception to the rule of anonymity, because nothing in the world of art is fixed: it is symbolized by the name of Mimar Sinan, one of the ever greatest architects the world has known, peer to Bramante or Michelangelo. He lived in Istanbul in the sixteenth century, the faithful servant of the Ottoman sultan Suleiman the Magnificent.

MAJOR WORKS AND MONUMENTS

Egypt, Cairo, Madrasah of Sultan Hasan
India, Agra, Taj Mahal mausoleum
Iran, Isfahan, Great Mosque
Iraq, Samarra, Great Mosque
Israel, Jerusalem, Dome of the Rock
Morocco, Fès, Kairaouine Mosque
Spain, Granada, Alhambra Palace
Spain, Cordoba, Great Mosque
Syria, Aleppo, Khusruwiyah Mosque, architect Mimar Sinan
Syria, Damascus, Great Mosque
Tunis, Kairouan, Great Mosque
Turkey, Edirne, Mosque of Selim II, architect Mimar Sinan
Turkey, Istanbul, Blue Mosque
Turkey, Istanbul, Mosque of Suleiman the Magnificent, architect Mimar Sinan

12. **Art or No Art**

The fall of the Roman Empire (476) signed the beginning of centuries of turbulence in the wide area of Western and Central Europe. Political instability, invasions, epidemics, migrations of entire peoples, wars, piracy on the seas and insecurity on the roads, stirring up and mixing of populations, languages, customs and creeds, all this offered unfavorable circumstances for the production of art. During those many centuries the center of European culture moved to the Eastern Roman (Byzantine or Greek) empire, with Constantinople as the decreasing Christian stronghold facing the expanding Islamic empires, with Cairo, Damascus, Bagdad, Isfahan and many other splendid cities. Further to the east, following the Silk Road, there lay the empires of India, China, Korea and Japan, the kingdoms of Cambodia, Myanmar, Thailand and Java and many more, all vast dominions where Buddhism was the best implanted religion. In these ages empires rose and fell in the Americas, as yet isolated from the Old World. In all those regions, though not free from natural and human disasters, art and technology developed to admirable heights, with stunning successes in many media. Pottery and jewelry, weavings and metalwork, miniatures and calligraphy, mosaics, sculpture and painting flourished as well as daring architecture. In comparison, the Christian West was poor and chaotic, divided and destabilized, backward and warring, an easy prey for devastating Huns and Goths, Vandals and Vikings. The era is called the Dark Ages because writing had become a relative exception and we know little of its history. In many aspects and in spite of brave impulses from the Church (Saint Patrick, Saint Columban,

Saint Boniface) and remarkable individual personalities (Justinian, Charlemagne), its civilization fell sometimes almost back into pre-history. It is from this "ground zero" that we have an opportunity to study the return of the arts.

Stability came back not before around the year 1000. Then West-ern European civilization, now known as the West, took off on its own for a thousand years. At that moment, its dominant and dis-tinguishing element was the Roman Catholic Church, a branch of the Christian religion. The strongest, most vital elements in the Church were the monastic orders, which had been rare strong-holds in the preceding turmoil, the Benedictine order in the first place. New (sub)orders came now into being: Cistercians, Car-thusians, Antonines, Premonstratensians and many others. Their greatest accomplishments were realized in the first half of the twelfth century when the abbey of Cluny reigned supreme over 1,600 sister institutions in Europe and the Cistercians could cele-brate ten to twenty daughter foundations per year.

Christian monks are solitary men living in groups. This contra-diction has been a powerful seed in a dry soil to make it fertile. Art often grows out of human paradox. It makes reason out of the irrational. The monks are the founding fathers of European culture. They claimed to be not of this world, and in fact they retreated far from society into the wilderness and lived in a closed (*cloister*) monastery, which was basically not more than a church plus some humble living quarters, surrounded by a wall. They lived a monotonous life according to an ascetic, inhumane rule, in poverty and isolation, working hard with their hands and head. They didn't speak, using their voice only to say, at precise hours of the day in unison with the brotherhood, holy lines from Latin Scripture in a pious form of recitation that slowly evolved into an almost obsessive chant. From this Gregorian chant will eventually grow European music. The monks condemned as sinful the body and its needs, food, comfort, sensuality, sexuality, greed, pride, anger, violence. They condemned the individual personality. They condemned art as luxury or idolatry. They tried to found a society on chant or prayer alone, excluding the visual arts.

Possible? Impossible! Here we see how art is inevitable and vital to the human kind. There is no human community life without art. But what is art? Art is the indomitable creative force that sprouts from life and formats human social activity. It overcomes death and decay and communicates essence; it permits humans to believe in the spirit and another life. Aren't those claims also Christian common places? In fact the Christian monks reinvented painting, sculpture, and architecture as if out of necessity. The junction of word (poetry, prayer) and image is indeed a definition of humanity, its origin and destiny.

In spite of intellectual resistance, art came back with new strength, in new forms and with new content. But not without roots. The monks, the learned men of their time, would throw the bridge from their present to the past in an urge of renascence. These pious Christians would assimilate the art of pagan Romans, take up or take in the idiom of heathen Vikings, Celts and Teutons, and develop a viable synthesis, a new interpretation of old forms, by giving them a new sense and a future. They built their churches according to new canons of austere durability, perfecting above all the art of *resonance*. Chanting to God was their goal in life; music as well as architecture transmitted the cosmic laws of harmony as an experience of space: oral, auditory, visual, and intellectual. As teachers, they renewed sculpture so as to conjugate history, legends and morals in a vivid style for the unlearned folks coming from far, the pilgrims. As scholars they would tirelessly study and copy the Gospels, writing in noble script on resistant parchment, embellished with remarkable restraint: it was the Word of God. Sober beauty had to serve the strict monastic rule, the keyword of which was humility.

The success of the monastic retreat from the world was immense: *in the world!* It reached from ethics to economics. The number of abbeys and monasteries grew exponentially, as well as the number of monks in the monasteries. Half of Europe, the poorest of continents, was transformed in an architect's or artist's studio. The art of building evolved to summits of perfection, drawing many skills in its following. The monks were like the nucleus of the atom, reserves of potential energy for the society. They initiated lasting reforms of agriculture, industry, justice, education, and healthcare. Women followed the men in separate houses, an early wave of social emancipation. Rarely in history have so large groups of men and women lived up so fervently to an unworldly ideal, sacrificing all that was not entirely destined to the spirit, refusing all that was not fundamental.

Whoever travels now in Romanesque France or Spain, Italy or Croatia, is struck by the *terrestrial* nature of this early art, speaking strongly to modern people: its powerful authenticity as manual work, the almost visible courage and perseverance, the human scale and grandeur, primitive and sublime at the same time. We learn here that to become spiritual, the human being has to recognize matter as its root and grow from it. The more one renounces the body, the more the body will make itself manifest. This is probably a universal law of art.

Success, alas, was the pitfall: a contradiction in monastic terms. The monasteries became rich, owners of land and capital, powerful, proud, and competitors, merciless competitors. They forgot the first line of the rule that said poverty. They lost their moral superiority, and the primacy in the arts was taken over by the cathedrals.

MAJOR WORKS AND MONUMENTS

Belgium, Nivelles, Benedictine Abbey of Saint Gertrude

Croatia, Zadar, Church of the Holy Trinity (chapel of bishop Saint Donatus)

Czech Republic, Milevsko, Premonstratensian Monastery

France, Chartreuse Mountain, *Grande Chartreuse* (head monastery of the Carthusian order)

France, Cluny, Benedictine Abbey (head monastery of the Cluniac sub-order)

France, Fontenay, Cistercian Abbey

France, Mont Saint-Michel, Benedictine Abbey

France, Pontigny, Cistercian Abbey

France, Sénanque, Cistercian Abbey

France, Tournus, Saint Philibert Benedictine Abbey

Germany, Aachen, Palatine Chapel (Charlemagne's church)

Germany, Andernach, Maria Laach, Benedictine Abbey

Ireland, Dingle Peninsula, Kilmalkedar Church

Italy, Forli, Benedictine Abbey of San Mercuriale

Italy, Monte Cassino, head monastery of the Benedictine Order

Spain, Emporda, Sant Miquel de Cuixa, Benedictine Abbey

Spain, Sastago, Royal Monastery of Our Lady of the Wheel, Cistercian Abbey

Turkey, Istanbul, Hagia Sophia church (now a mosque)

13. **Art Outside or Inside**

ROMANESQUE   **WESTERN EUROPE**   **1000–1200**

The classical civilization had cultivated the outside, in society and art. The Parthenon, the Temple of Jerusalem, even the Pyramids were dwellings of the gods; men stayed out. They stood like rocks above the middle (and the muddle) of the society. They were pure symbols, and as such only visible from the outside. The statues of Venus, Apollo, even Ramses, even Caesar are mere bodies. The gods themselves were too powerful to have an inner life. They outlined the ideal that people are defined by the outside: physical appearance, social status, action.

During the growing insecurity of the first millennium, under the pressure of new religions and philosophy, the self-image of man turned, so to say, outside in. The spirit that used to be in the air or in the stone entered in us; it was not anymore in the mask or the statue but in our heart, and therefore even more invisible. The interior man became the true one. The monk was not a body, but a soul. The soul was the good part of man, while the body was vile, evil, risk, and ruin. In that world view, woman was the danger, the temptation, she reminded a man of his body, she was his moral weakness: some theologians would go as far as to refuting her a soul. Sexuality was a vice, celibacy and virginity were virtues. The central message of the Church was the cult of the Virgin Mary.

Preceded in the East by Byzantine and Moslem culture, Romanesque was the art that drew the conclusions of this slow mental evolution in Western society. How faithfully do our hands follow our mental representation of the human being! From now on sacred

architecture (and there was no other) became the art of con-
structing insides. To start with this meant conceiving the room for
praise: within the sturdy church walls, like in the chest of a person, the glorification of the divine being must sound and resound
interminably. Far from singing a song, the chant was an inner
(meditative) experience; not the mouth but the ear was its instrument, infinitely enhanced by the acoustic qualities of solid stone
barrel vaults functioning as sound boards for tones and under-
tones. Mute construction matter (mud and stone) was elevated
by the monks' hands and tools, converted into singing (vibrating)
heavenly vaults. So it was for the heavy earthly body: elevated on
complex modulations of the Gregorian air, it was changed into a
pure angelic spirit joining the invisible God.

Outside the Church is no salvation: for us a clerical pretension, for
them the reality of a concrete building and an artistic device. The
church was (symbolically) modeled on the body of Man, image of
God. Its forms, beauty and sense, were found inside, scent and
music and prayer and light, just like the beauty and sense of a
human being is of the heart: faith, compassion, morality, hope,
not muscles, clothes, or even health.

The same emphasis invaded sculpture and painting. The supreme
goal of the outside form became the evocation of strong inner
life, either by anatomically impossible torsions and proportions
or by severe material sobriety. Graphic or vivid linear patterns
succeeded in animating whichever surface. The colors were stark
and contrasting. Art gave life to the inanimate stone, sense to the
void parchment, purity to the impure matter. Copying the outside
world never sufficed, or worse, it was a non-sense, and a non-
beauty. Art transcended the visual appearances. A new world
would replace them, the life of which was already in us and art
could show us.

71

Vast sculptural compositions were placed at the entrance of the churches, like guardians between the outside and the inside, symbolizing the exit of the world and the entrance into paradise. They showed Christ descending from the heavens as the universal judge. They implied a questioning of conscience to those who entered. Inside, not only in the abbeys but also now in parish churches and cathedrals, the construction of which multiplied rapidly, the capitals of the pillars, empty once, were filled with biblical stories and holy legends. Narrative frescoes began to cover the walls, just like in the gospel books and psalters the text was underlined by drawings in the margins. These illuminated manuscripts, rarely opened, normally closed like a secret, must be seen as the works most valued as art.

Western man has never given up this belief in an inner life as superior to the outer body. Even in our time, in spite of the violence of economic and social systems, and of cynical ideology, we honor strongly the idea. One of its symptoms we call *equality,* of race or gender or religion, something we situate in our (invisible) inside. Our (sometimes misplaced) *respect* for whatever artistic expression is also a result of it, inherent to our values, like freedom of speech.

One might argue that the dichotomy of *out* and *in* is the leitmotiv of a thousand years of art. Form versus content, reason versus emotion, social versus individual, they are all variations on this simple theme.

MAJOR WORKS AND MONUMENTS

Croatia, Poreč, Saint Euphrasius Basilica

France, Autun, Saint-Lazare Cathedral

France, Le Thoronet, Cistercian Abbey

France, Moissac, Benedictine Abbey

France, Vézelay, Benedictine Abbey of St Mary-Magdalen
Great Britain, Durham, Saint Cuthbert Cathedral
Ireland, Dublin, Trinity College Library, *Book of Kells*
Italy, Pisa, Duomo (Cathedral Saint Mary of the Assumption) and Bell Tower
Italy, Ravenna, Church of San Vitale
Italy, Sicily, Monreale, Cathedral Saint Mary of the Assumption
Italy, Venice, Saint Mark's Basilica
Italy, Verona, Benedictine Abbey of San Zeno, bronze doors
Portugal, Lisbon, Cathedral (Sé)
Spain, Barcelona, National Museum of Catalonia, Romanesque frescos
Spain, Ripoll, Benedictine Abbey
Spain, Santiago de Compostela, Pilgrimage Church

14. Art and Faith

The monks of Christendom imagined bringing earth up into heaven; their followers, the bishops, believed in bringing heaven down to earth. The first demonstrated and dominated the laws of physics; the second challenged and transcended them. The first bent their heads down and heard the voice of angels; the second turned their eyes up and saw them.

Gothic is a set of building techniques, then a style, and in the end an overall artistic performance. The pointed arch, omnipresent sculpture, and stained glass are its most typical expressions. It is the glorious product of growing political order and relative peace in Europe under the guidance of a powerful unifying religion, the Roman Catholic Church. Gothic architecture first appeared when the excellent abbot Suger had his abbey church renovated at Saint-Denis (out of Paris, France) in 1136-44. Its classic phase started before 1200 in the provinces around the French capital and lasted until the end of the reign of King Louis IX, who had the *Sainte-Chapelle* erected around 1250. Famous are Notre-Dame, Paris, Notre-Dame, Chartres, and Bourges, Reims, Amiens, Troyes, Beauvais, all cathedrals dedicated to the Virgin Mary, except for Troyes. At that moment the style had spread all over Europe. England was the second great country of Gothic. Here we must mention at least the cathedrals of Canterbury, Salisbury and Wells. But from Norway to Spain, and from Ireland to Poland the new style had been adopted (and adapted) and left masterpieces of architecture and art.

Two generations later the apparent Roman Catholic unity broke down into rivalry between provinces and states. With regional particularities ever more prominent, Western Europe continued to build dynamically on the Gothic foundations, and even in the Gothic spirit, adhering to it as they did to Roman Catholic theology, with as many differing interpretations and varieties of the dogma. Every city and town had (and often still has) a remarkable Gothic church (not always the cathedral) in its center. Let me mention just a few more cities with such a stunning building as its identity and pride: in Germany Cologne or Magdeburg (or Ulm!), in Italy Florence or Milan (or Orvieto!), in France Strasbourg or Rouen (or Albi!), in Spain Toledo or Barcelona (or Granada!), and Prague and Krakow and Ghent and Trondheim and Dublin and Utrecht and Edinburgh and Antwerp. . .

Faith is the conviction that man can defy the human condition and invert its laws. Faith against all rational odds is a central thesis of the Christian creed, claiming a virginal birth, the resurrection of the dead, a universal judgment, the end of time, eternal love. Faith accepts saints, angels and miracles. How can an ideology of the unbelievable be transferred into a building technique and take form? That is the essence of the Gothic enterprise: to embody the spirit of faith, or to spiritualize the worldly reality.

In order to challenge the laws of physics Gothic art takes full advantage of only two basic devices.

First, the invention and exclusive use of the pointed arch, forming the typical cross-vault, not only allowed stability to very high structures, but enhanced the optical effects of height, depth and lightness. Second, throwing important structural elements to the outside (*flying buttresses*) allowed the stone walls to be replaced by glass, determining the inside experience. The result was that to the eye the bishop's church ("cathedral") elevated itself into infinite height carried by colored light, not stone. Simple and beyond comprehension. Something like a monumental miracle, indeed.

Faith is a potent human faculty and a universal phenomenon; it was not invented during the European Middle Ages. Gothic Europe offers a clear example of its artistic impact and possibilities, when the economy and technology of every country seemed to have chosen as its supreme goal to surpass the modesty of reason in the name of holy architecture (the time for palaces and town halls would come, but only a century later) and when the names of the formidable builders and decorators stayed in humble shadows. It is not a unique case. The archeological wonders of the lost city of Angkor, in northern Cambodia, fill us with the same admiration mixed with awe. They were built when the Buddhist Khmer Empire was at the height of its power, curiously coinciding with the European Middle Ages, between 1000 and 1500. Equally in the 11th to 14th century thousands of temples, pagodas and monasteries were constructed in Bagan, the capital of the Kingdom of Bagan, in modern Myanmar. Even older by two hundred years are the astounding Borobudur Temple Compounds in the Indonesian island of Java. In West China, in the region surrounding the Silk Road oasis Dunhuang, during a thousand years a thousand temples were carved by communities of monks in the grottoes, sanctuaries to contain sculptures, frescoes and manuscripts. These are examples between many extraordinary others, reminding us of the Buddhist contribution to the architectural and artistic creations in the name of faith. In the Islamic world we should point to the Safavid Empire stretching over what is roughly Iran today. During the period coinciding with the Renaissance and Baroque in Western Europe, Shiism was *Jihad-wise,* merciless that is, implanted there; then prosperity grew with relative peace and the cities, especially Isfahan, were changed into magnificent places with not only palaces and parks, but mosques and madrasahs all over. Also in the Near-East, during an even longer period and covering a wider sphere, including Eastern Europe and Northern Africa, the Ottoman Empire, defender of the Sunni faith did the same, providing Europe with a dream of the Blessed Orient. Irrational faith, not rational political, social or juridical constructions were able to inspire artists, architects and engineers and give concrete form to a spiritual ideal as a reality of the human being.

Faith, though, didn't disappear with the decline of religions as the powerful center of societies. In our time it is less destined to the crowd and more to the individual. We don't limit faith to religious experience. We situate it in the psychological rather than the social field. It is not imposed from above, but infused from within. Our time preaches *faith in one-self*. Maybe we can say that the modern artist is the best representative of this irrational creed that is however fundamental for our time. He or she needs it in great doses, certainly. We sometimes call it the sacred fire. Standing before an artwork as spectators we are always invited to look for signs of this complex mixture of hope and belief in life. Faith beyond reason and faith against all odds are basic elements of the energy the artist can transfer in a work. The art lover finds here a strong indication of authenticity or inspiration.

MAJOR WORKS AND MONUMENTS

Apart from works and monuments mentioned in the chapter.

Austria, Vienna, Stephansdom (St Stephen's cathedral)
Belgium, Brussels, Cathedral Saint Michael

Cambodia, Siem Reap, Angkor Wat, Buddhist temple complex
China, Dunhuang, *Mogao Caves of the Thousand Buddhas*

Czech Republic, Kutna Hora, St Barbara's Cathedral

France, Avignon, Palace of the Popes

France, Laon, Notre Dame Cathedral

France, Paris, Abbey church of Saint-Denis, choir and ambulatory

Germany, Bamberg, Saint Peter and Saint George Cathedral

Germany, Naumburg, Saint Peter and Saint Paul Cathedral

Germany, Trier, Liebfrauenkirche (Church of Our Lady)

Great Britain, London, Westminster Abbey

Great Britain, Cambridge, King's College Chapel

Indonesia, Central Java, Borobudur Buddhist Temple Compounds

Italy, Venice, Church of Saint Francis (Frari)

Myanmar, Bagan, Buddhist temples and pagodas

Netherlands, Haarlem, Grand Church (Saint Bavo Cathedral)

Poland, Torun, Church of Saint James

South Korea, Seoul, National Museum of Korea, *Gyeongcheonsa Pagoda*

Spain, Burgos, Cathedral of Saint Mary

Spain, Girona (Gerona), Cathedral of Saint Mary

Switzerland, Basel, Minster (Cathedral of Saints Henry and Kunigonde)

15. **Art and Vision**

The profound human desire to see with the eyes what no eye has seen, to see beyond the limits of nature, to see into the dwellings of the gods, was the focus and privilege of Gothic man, whose successes were greatest in the arts. The medium was stained glass in vast architectural settings. With it the artist bound the light, which is symbolically speaking *the matter of the spirit*. Artistically speaking we recognize a *tour de force*.

Originally glass was not, like ours, white (colorless), or flat, or clear; it was colored, of irregular thickness and shape, and full of bubbles: it was blown. The Romans, marvelous craftsmen, used it for vases, and the early Christians as well as the Muslims used it in their sanctuaries in small windows. Really great use comes with gothic architecture and its huge glass surfaces. Kept in place by an iron grid and thick lead lining, one could not see through it, although the light could penetrate from outside in deep red or blue or yellow hues. Hence, it was not used to see more or better, as you were probably taught. No, it continued to be quite dark inside the church, rather more than less, for a good reason: to provoke an awe-inspiring experience, a mystery beyond words, as sure as does the rainbow breaking through the darkest clouds. It served uniquely those who were inside the building, the happy few (though this was the major part of the community), leaving those on the outside deprived of it (the ex-communicated). And while white-draped boys would sing in high-pitched voices, the priest in his sermon would compare the church to the New Jerusalem "descending from God." This was a Christian simile of the other-worldly heavens.

In prophecy and poetry of all religions, the heavens are described in terms of gold and precious stones. The gothic cathedral had the ambition to come close to its material realization. Here the masons and glass blowers reached out for emeralds and rubies, topaz and sapphires multiplied to the infinite. Set in deep and rich colors, illuminated by the sun rising in the east, like a blessing fire, the gathering of the saints and angels around the Virgin Mary and her God son above the community of the faithful became a more than visual experience. The crowds must have believed at moments to cross the borders of the real and to receive a vision of another world.

This experience of *rapture*, this miraculous event reported in so many legends of the Middle Ages and Renaissance, every ordinary tourist can go for it now on every ordinary day of the year. A partial explanation lies in the fabric of our eye and the particularity of the medium. Stained, that is, painted colorful glass is the only art technique in which the subject is visible by light coming from the back. Normally, the eye sees an object thanks to the reflection of the light falling on it. It allows the brain to fix the relative position of both object and observer. In the case of the semi-opaque stained glass, if the staring eye doesn't move, as is proper in the church service, it sees the reflection being taken over and replaced by an emanation at the source (the object), through which colored light invades the space. This results in faint trembling (instability), enhanced by the property of color to vibrate in specific undulation, red appears closer than blue or green. (Don't wink, you'd better sit down on a chair; the saints of old fell on their knees, keeping their eyes fixed on the light, not always keeping their feet on the ground.) The brain hesitates, unable to determine distances in the dark; space seems to disappear, interference happens of far and near, of solid and void; the effect in us is loss of spatial reference, confusion, or euphoria. In strong versions we give it the names of *hypnosis* or *hallucination*. Religions name it *visions*. The brain discovers a reality disconnected with the one it knows so well; it may settle in it for a while. The outer eye connects to an inner eye and becomes one with it. Physiologically speaking it is not unrelated to the dream, to meditation or to the mystical trance. A truly psychic experience. The reality of art is always a seesaw movement between the physical and the psychological; but hardly ever as subtle and persuasive as in a stained glass environment.

The fascination of especially young people for hallucinatory and psychedelic experiences outside of a religious context is characteristic for the modern age. Our time proposes quite typically pills and powders and needles, all chemistry, to provoke "mind-blowing" effects on our consciousness. Nightclubs add violent destabilizing light effects. It might finally be cheaper and safer to go to a Gothic cathedral. More peaceful too. One would find out that the arts propose us an involvement of the eye and the brain that makes drugs quite superfluous (with possible satisfaction of another type).

After centuries of decline, the love for stained glass came back in the nineteenth century when the Neo-Gothic building style became fashionable. Around 1900 it saw the rise of one of America's greatest early modern artists: Louis Comfort Tiffany. A second revival took place after World War II, when twentieth-century artists reinterpreted the monumental potential of the medium. It has given the world some of its most moving modern monuments. Marc Chagall, of Jewish origin, deserves here a special mention;

stained glass was the lamp in his spiritual relighting of Europe after Nazi destruction and holocaust: whole sets in Zurich, Metz, Paris, Nice, several in Germany, as well as in the United Nations Building in New York, and Israel. More recently, important state commissions have been given to contemporary artists in historic monuments and other venerable buildings to accompany restoration work. The windows by Pierre Soulages in the Romanesque pilgrimage church of Conques have been the touchstone for public approval of such daring interventions.

MAJOR WORKS AND MONUMENTS

Apart from works and monuments mentioned in the chapter.

France, Blois, St. Louis Cathedral, Jan Dibbets, *stained glass*

France, Chartres, Notre Dame Cathedral

France, Paris, Sainte-Chapelle

France, Strasbourg, Notre Dame Cathedral

France, Troyes, Cathedral

France, Vence, Henri Matisse, *Chapel of the Rosary*

Great Britain, Canterbury, Cathedral of the Holy Saviour, Becket Miracle Windows

Great Britain, Lincoln, Cathedral of the Blessed Virgin Mary, Ward and Nixon, *re-glazed east window*

Great Britain, Oxford, Merton College Church

Great Britain, York, Cathedral of St. Peter

Germany, Berlin, Kaiser Wilhelm Memorial Church, Gabriel Loire, *stained glass*

Germany, Mainz, Stephanskirche (Church of St. Stephen), Marc Chagall, *stained glass*

Israel, Jerusalem, Hadassah University Medical Center, Abbell Synagogue, Marc Chagall, *12 stained glass windows*

Spain, León, Cathedral of Santa Maria de la Regla

USA, New Haven, NJ, Yale University, Louis Comfort Tiffany, *the Education Window*

PART TWO

16. **Art and Rebirth**

EARLY RENAISSANCE   **ITALY**   **1410–1500**

In the middle of the Gothic world, and long before it ended, the germ of a new world began to sprout in a rich and powerful city in Italy, Florence. There was nothing unconscious about it. The inhabitants realized soon that after long economic and political successes (and sometimes serious blows, the greatest one being the plague of 1348, called the Black Death), their city was exceptional in history by giving birth to a new art. In fact, they used other words. They said it gave *rebirth* (*Rinascimento*, or Renaissance) to *old* art. Old, or ancient, meant Roman. They saw their city as a new Rome, or a new Athens. This return to a period considered classical was not a rare phenomenon as such in the history of civilizations; its success was. The thousand years between the fall of old Rome and the birth of the new one were described as a decadent, dark and barbarous middle period, middle ages. We still use the words they invented out of city pride, even if we know that the middle ages were not always dark. On the contrary, the Middle Ages had seen several Roman revivals, in politics and arts. Only think of the *emperor* Charlemagne and the Holy Roman Empire of the German Nation. And think of Romanesque art. In fact, in the eyes of the Middle Ages, Rome had never died, never disappeared. The head of the *Roman* Catholic Church, the Pope was still there, and governing; the ancient empire was represented by its last religion. Now the Florentines made it clear that Rome was dead, that the Pope was only pope and that Italian as a language was not Latin. They defended the idea that in order to know and maybe rebuild the greatness of Rome, they had to explore and study it as if unknown: re-publish and re-interpret the Latin authors, re-discover the remaining architectural and sculptural monuments. They did it with passion, rigor and objectivity. The first movement, in the fourteenth century, was literary, we call it Humanism; its greatest names are Dante, Petrarch and Boccaccio. The second movement, the Renaissance of the fifteenth century, centered on art and architecture: the first classical buildings saw the light, easily to be distinguished from everything gothic in the rest of the continent. We know the builders: Brunelleschi, Michelozzo, Alberti. The first classic looking free-standing (!) sculptures (statues) appear on the outside of churches. We know the names of their masters: Donatello, Ghiberti.

The first, *Trecento (1300-s)* Humanist movement had been, let's not forget it, magnificent in the arts, too. In all of Italy the art of fresco and panel painting was revived. Its revolutionary masters were Duccio and Giotto, Simone Martini and the Lorenzetti brothers. In spite of their breakthrough quality, we classify them as late Gothic, as its architecture certainly was. One of the reasons is that Italy was not alone, then; other parts of Europe participated in the progress. Notably Bohemia with its blooming capital Prague, where the Holy Roman Emperor Charles IV had his palace built and spanned the famous bridge over the Vltava (Moldau) river, Bohemia with its superb castles and churches, also contributed to the history of painting. The towering genius is here Master Theodoric. Another reason is that the most prestigious commissions could very well concern other media than painting, notably splendid illuminated books or vast suites of tapestry. However, the break with the past is consummated in Florence in the fifteenth century, in Italian: the *Quattrocento*. That is where History has the new times begin. The arts show it clearly.

It started as an artistic demographic phenomenon: never had there been so many painter's and sculptor's workshops, never so many commissions in one country at the same time as then in Italy. It was a matter of cities and the competition between them: Florence, headed by three generations of the Medici banking family, took the lead, but Siena, the eternal rival, followed with Urbino, Arezzo, Pisa in Tuscany; then Venice, with Padua, Verona, Mantua, Ferrara in the Veneto; as well as Milan in Lombardy, with Pavia and Bergamo; now Genoa, Bologna, Rome and Naples couldn't stay behind. Italy became again the uncontested center of European art, architecture, literature, gardening, good manners and general wellbeing. Tragically it also became the center of warfare, destroying much of the new found beauty, dividing what should be united, weakening what should be strengthened and so making it a tempting prey for rising foreign powers: France and Spain.

The Italian rediscovery and re-esteem of the classical past played a major role in the building of a specific Western European culture. It functioned as an incubator and catalysis in thought and action alike. A human-centered world view, independent science, freedom of conscience, followed by ever growing freedom for literature, philosophy and the arts are in our eyes the positive characteristics of it; others less so: the lack of respect for foreign cultures and subsequent abuse of power.

American education has always flirted with the Italian Renaissance. No city in Europe (apart maybe from Paris) is as popular as Florence, and for many students Donatello, Botticelli, or Leonardo are almost familiar names. The last one, under the name Da Vinci, could even become the character of a bestselling thriller. More seriously, the American Revolution was nourished by ideas of Renaissance, that is, the return to Roman republican values and architecture. Quite surprisingly, you'd say, the typical 19th century American college campus witnessed a revival of Gothic architecture, the style of those "dark" Middle Ages; we find it back in the graduation ceremonies, too.

The Renaissance, then, represents the intellectual move that marks the beginning of a new and original insight in the arts, one that would last for five centuries. From essentially manual the society began to see them as products of the mind: art as a form of poetry. From a laborer the artist became a thinker. The artist, not the customer or commissioner, became the premier person responsible of the work: he (sometimes *she,* now!) signs it. Even if this social change for him (and her) was very slow and was never complete, artist and artwork entered into a long process of emancipation.

These general remarks should make you understand that we are still in many ways the direct sons and daughters of the Renaissance. It is significant that from this period on we begin to say that art works look *real*. That is the more interesting, since the artists who made them were rather in search for an *ideal*. There is reason to keep in mind this confusion of terms, because it feeds our notion of reality and our view of art. The following lessons will add thoughts to that central question.

MAJOR WORKS AND MONUMENTS

Czech Republic, Karlstejn Castle, Chapel of the Holy Cross, Master Theodoric, *Prophets, Saints and Angels*

France, Angers, Château, Jean Bondol (painter) and Nicolas Bataille (weaver), *Apocalypse Tapestry*

France, Avignon, Palace of the Popes, Simone Martini *e.a.*, frescoes in the Pope's apartments

Italy, Assisi, Basilica of Saint Francis d'Assisi, Giotto and workshop, *Life of Saint Francis*

Italy, Florence, Baptistery Saint John the Baptist, Lorenzo Ghiberti, *bronze doors*

Italy, Florence, Brunelleschi, arch., *Capella Pazzi* (Chapel of the Pazzi family)

Italy, Florence, Brunelleschi, arch., *Church of Santo Spirito*

Italy, Florence, Brunelleschi, arch., Cathedral Santa Maria dei Fiori (Duomo), *Cupola*

Italy, Florence, Church of Orsanmichele, Donatello, *Saint George, Saint Mark*

Italy, Florence, Giotto, arch., Cathedral Santa Maria dei Fiori (Duomo), *Bell Tower*

Italy, Florence, Michelozzo, arch., *Medici Palace*

Italy, Florence, Museo del Bargello, Donatello, *Saint Mary-Magdalene*

Italy, Padua, Giotto (architect and painter), *Scrovegni Chapel*

Italy, Padua, Donatello, *Equestrian Statue of Gattamelata*

Italy, Rimini, Leon Battista Alberti, arch., Tempio Malatestiano, *façade*

Italy, Siena, Museo Civico, Simone Martini, *Maestà (Madonna with Saints and Angels)*

Italy, Siena, Museo Civico, Ambrogio Lorenzetti, *Allegories of Good and Bad Government*

Italy, Siena, Museo dell'Opera Metropolitana del Duomo, Duccio, *Maestà (Madonna with Saints and Angels)*

17. **Art and Illusion 1**
(Perspective)

EARLY AND HIGH RENAISSANCE   **ITALY**   **1425–1525**

The most widely acclaimed discovery of the Florentines was and is linear perspective. It is a mathematical (geometric) formula and an explanation of our vision of space, of our capacity to see distances. Filippo Brunelleschi, the young sculptor and architect, conceived around 1415 an elegant experiment to expose the principles of it. The most important one: parallel lines, when they recede, visually converge into a vanishing point, situated on the horizon; the horizon line is the collection of all vanishing points. The cause of this is the spherical construction of the eye, functioning not unlike a convex mirror. Objects look smaller when they are further away and their form adapts to the angle under which the eye sees it: a circle becomes an ellipse; this is called *foreshortening.* Perspective is the way of our eye and brain to *measure* objects and the void in between. It gives us a feeling of control, security, balance and well-being. The new theory offered itself as a practical device in line drawing and in the building trade, for instance, a rational means to meet the diminishing proportions of motionless things in the distance and the relations between them. It was soon adopted by painters and sculptors as an unrivaled and quasi magical method to open the third dimension in flat artworks and obtain objective unity in the suggested space. The young and ambitious Masaccio was the first to paint a monumental fresco, the *Holy Trinity* (a most appropriate subject) in the church of Santa Maria Novella, as a superb demonstration of perspective's inherent possibilities for the arts in the future. During a century brilliant Italian and foreign artists would explore its secrets and joys. Famous masterpieces are due to scrupulous research in these matters by such masters as Piero della Francesca, Leonardo da Vinci, Albrecht Dürer or Hans Holbein the Younger.

Perspective is without any doubt a powerful tool to render reality, and still today the public, you and I, can't help but divide the *history* of art in two: before and after its invention. Here we draw also the line in the *geography* of art: the West and the Rest. We often hear people (maybe you too) say that only since the Renaissance (that means since the invention of perspective) a painting looks *real,* or *true.* And you continue in the same phrase by saying it is *beautiful,* maybe because of a certain feeling of security and control. You are in good company; the Italians of the Renaissance said similar things. They were the first in Europe to seek in art primarily beauty; they would even demand it. The knowledge of perspective was vital in their eyes, as they were convinced that beauty came with good measurements and correct proportions. Now think about the word *real,* just mentioned and compare it to the fact, easily understood, that linear perspective is the first and still the best method to paint *illusions,* that is, eye-deceivers (in art the word is *trompe-l'oeil*). For centuries art's occupation has been to fool the eye. The public liked it, and still does. It was there, where the artist's skill seemed most striking. The better an artist fools us, the more he or she pleases us. Art looks real, when it is... fake. How exciting to delude or to be deluded! A painting is a true lie!

The artists since the Renaissance were manual workers *and* intellectual workers. The arts, and the artists with them, had always been close to the body of *knowledge* of a society, but in the Renaissance they moved to the *sciences* like mathematics, philosophy, linguistics, archeology or astrology. They included in their art humanist rationality, which is sometimes, believe me, quite obscure for us. In short, the arts gained in *figurative* representation as much as in *abstract* reasoning.

But here is again the surprise. The artists, great practitioners of the sciences that made us understand nature, used them to confound us. The more art is "real," you mean "figurative", the more its deeper meaning is hidden in symbols, allegories and metaphors. As always, the arts ask from the art lover (we say now art appreciator) a total investment of the person, head, and heart—don't forget the head. However attractive, Renaissance art is intellectual and its beauty is not sentimental. The visual *illusion* is an intelligent adventure, often a sacred one, sometimes close to a mystic *riddle*, offered to the sharpest intellect to solve, which alone is capable to match the ingenuity of the artist. More than before the artists seem to say: you don't see what you see, however real it looks to your eye. So make your eye think.

Modern art abandoned the concept of illusion as an artistic device: in the name of truth. It came back in disguise. For the Renaissance and Baroque, the magic of perspective had been the way to make the impossible possible. For the Surrealists, Dali, Magritte, Man Ray, Escher, it was a way to make the possible impossible. And Op-Art teased the eye to destabilize the brain. Realism is not dead, though. Illusion is not dead, either. It slipped away from the art scene to become a popular game. *Photoshop* can be highly amusing and is easily available for everyone. In a more *virtuoso* vein, gifted street artists exploit with surprising skill the principles of linear perspective in extreme foreshortenings, producing stunning *anamorphosis* art on the streets of our shopping centers. Others stand motionless as a bronze sculpture—until they suddenly walk away, with a handful of dollars.

MAJOR WORKS AND MONUMENTS

Austria, Vienna, Albertina *e.a.,* Albrecht Dürer, *Drawing a Nude with a Perspective Device,* woodcut

Escher, M.C., *Ascending and Descending* (lithograph)

Great Britain, London, National Gallery, Hans Holbein the Younger, *The Ambassadors*

Great Britain, London, National Gallery, Paolo Uccello, *Battle of San Romano*

Italy, Florence, Baptistery Saint John the Baptist, Lorenzo Ghiberti, *Isaac and His Sons*

Italy, Florence, Church of Santa Maria del Carmine, Masaccio, frescoes of the *Brancacci Chapel*

Italy, Florence, Church of Sant'Apollonia, Andrea del Castagno, *Last Supper*

Italy, Florence, Convent of San Marco, Domenico Ghirlandaio, *Last Supper*

Italy, Florence, Uffizi Gallery, Paolo Uccello, *Perspective drawing of a Chalice*

Italy, Mantua, Ducal Palace, Andrea Mantegna, *Camera degli Sposi*

Italy, Milano, Pinacoteca di Brera, Piero della Francesca, *Enthroned Madonna and Saints*

Italy, Milano, Pinacoteca di Brera, Andrea Mantegna, *Dead Christ*

Italy, Siena, Cathedral Saint Mary of the Assumption, Donatello, *Feast of Herod*

Italy, Urbino, Galleria Nazionale delle Marche, Piero della Francesca, *Flagellation of Christ*

Man Ray, *Demain* (silver gelatin print)

Netherlands, Amsterdam, Rijksmuseum, Pieter Saenredam, *Church of Saint Odulphus, Assendelft*

18. Art as Oil Painting

EARLY RENAISSANCE   **FLANDERS**   **1425–1500**

When they leave the Middle Ages behind, the visual arts address themselves more and more to the eye. This seems a tautological error (like "the circle is more and more round"), but it isn't— it underlines that there must be a history of seeing. We don't see as our forefathers. It brings to our attention that since the Renaissance the eye becomes slowly but certainly the dominating sense of the human animal, the privileged key to science, reason, knowledge and truth. This might well be exemplified by the growing esteem of the society for the *visual* arts and artists. We begin to know artists' names, lives, opinions and (artistic) intentions. Amidst the visual arts painting becomes the leading form of expression, the purely visual art, leaving behind the finally more tactile sculpture. Within the domain of painting itself, oil on panel or canvas establishes prominence over all the other techniques, putting in place a hierarchy among the different media. It gained apparently a greater common denominator of sheer visibility, public value and private commodity than its competitors: oil would be closer to the spectator than the monumental *fresco*, more intimate in design, more subtle and smooth of surface than costly *tapestry*, more resistant in time than *pen and ink*, more generous to the crowd than precious *book illumination*, more comfortable to handle than *tempera,* infinitely richer in color than any of these and finally more lucrative for the salesman than all the others together. Even today, now everything is different (people say), a majority of the public, when hearing the word *art*, still thinks (if it thinks at all) of an oil-painting on canvas, in a frame.

The triumphal march of oil painting started in Flanders, in the same years that saw the first use of linear perspective in Florence, c. 1425. The authoritative artist here is Jan van Eyck from Bruges; his epoch-making master piece *The Mystic Lamb* is in the Ghent cathedral (showing in four steps the history of humankind from the first to the last paradise, again a most appropriate subject). Since long painters had tried to use oil of one kind or another as a binder for the colors, but only Jan van Eyck seems to have solved the crucial problem of making the oil dry (*the siccative secret*). The slowly drying paint made it possible to work with extreme precision in many layers. Technical secrets of this kind were kept by the masters like a copyright, and even today's research is not always able to crack their code. The brilliant genius of Jan van Eyck made good use of his discovery. Speaking about the inquisitive eye, maybe never in human history art has gone so far in the meticulous representation of the observable world. The unique transparency of the pristine linseed oil, binding the unmingled pigments that lend their subtle color to a shining palette for even shaded subjects, gave to painting the glory of a stainless mirror and the most precious stones. In one stroke, if I may use this expression, Flanders became a leading center of painting, the only rival to Italy. Besides Van Eyck, who had a workshop in Bruges, when he did not lead diplomatic missions for his powerful lord, the archduke Philip the Good of Burgundy, there was Robert Campin, better known as the Master of Flémalle, in Tournai; Roger van der Weyden, the famous painter of Brussels; Hugo van der Goes in Ghent; Geertgen tot Sint-Jans in Haarlem and many others in the proud cities of the Low Countries. These Flemish Primitives, as the world knows them now, had the right product for a new demand: small, extremely refined panels for private homes or chapels. Even their rare monumental size works kept the intimacy and density of book illustration, an art they kept supremacy in, too. Modest size devotion pieces, often showing contemporary home and church interiors, portable altar pieces and portraits for the prosperous burghers of the growing towns became the specialty and fame of Flemish studios.

From here oil painting started its conquest of Western Europe and of monumentality, via France, Germany, Switzerland, and Venice, to Rome, Naples, and Spain. The emotional potential of its rich color scheme was soon put to profit by new masters for generations to come. The school of Venice gained, thanks to the Bellini brothers, new prominence in Italy, which would last for the next three centuries. Its most impressive deed would be Tintoretto's performance in the Scuola di San Rocco; this unequaled enterprise, realized between 1564 and 1587, is to oil what the Sistine Chapel is to fresco. Oil painting was also the material basis of that sudden eruption of artistic genius, called the German Renaissance lead by Albrecht Dürer. Its greatest work, and one of the greatest of all time, is here the Issenheim altarpiece forged by Matthias Grünewald. Everywhere in Germany, Poland, Switzerland, Austria, France we can admire daring altarpieces that made the wall frescoes look pale. Only in Italy this last technique would continue to produce masterpieces and to lead the arts. Elsewhere oil completed its takeover around 1600, when canvas had practically replaced the wood panel. Its hegemony lasted some three centuries, so that in common speech "a canvas" became almost synonymous for any picture notwithstanding its technique. Oil painting has accompanied the long and spectacular adventure of *eye-centered* European thought and action.

Around 1900 scientific progression ruined the European habits of absolute confidence in the eye. Euclidian mathematics and traditional physics lost their authority. In the same period the arts shook off the yoke of the centralizing and hierarchal disciplines of both perspective and oils. Like the sciences, the visual arts took their distance from the eye, often trifling and scoffing at it, as if they celebrated the liberation from long slavery. In the past these "despots," oil paint and perspective, had given birth to the masterpieces of a civilization. Only think of Veronese, Velázquez, Vermeer, or Vigée-Lebrun; or, if you prefer, Raphael, Rubens, Rembrandt, or Rachel Ruysch.

It is not a rare fact that a civilization selects one or two artistic techniques among many others to transmit its spirit best. The media are a culture's honor. In Gothic art it was stained glass and miniature (book illumination). Byzantine art chose mosaic. We see how ceramics have always been considered a most noble art in China and Japan, a minor one in Europe; lacquer even more so, unknown to European traditions. Those Far Eastern countries painted in ink on silk; oil on canvas was not only unknown to them, it would have been considered extremely rude.

MAJOR WORKS AND MONUMENTS

Austria, Vienna, Academy of Fine Arts, Hieronymus Bosch, *Last Judgment*

Belgium, Antwerp, Museum voor Schone Kunsten, Jean Fouquet, *Madonna and Child*

Belgium, Bruges, Groeningemuseum, Jan van Eyck, *Madonna with Canon Joris van der Paele*

Belgium, Bruges, Sint-Janshospitaal, Memling Museum, Hans Memling, *Shrine of Saint Ursula*

Belgium, Louvain, church of St. Peter, Dieric Bouts, *Last Supper*

France, Beaune, Hôtel Dieu, Roger van der Weyden, *Last Judgment*

France, Château de Chantilly, Paul, Jean and Herman de Limbourg, *Très Riches Heures du Duc de Berry*

France, Colmar, Dominican Church, Martin Schongauer, *Madonna in a Rose Arbor*

France, Colmar, Musée Unterlinden, Matthias Grünewald, *Issenheim Altarpiece*

France, Paris, Musée du Louvre, Jan van Eyck, *Madonna with Chancellor Nicolas Rolin*

France, Villeneuve-lès-Avignon, Musée Pierre de Luxembourg, Enguerrand Quarton, *Coronation of the Virgin*

Germany, Berlin, Gemäldegalerie, Petrus Christus, *Portrait of a Young Woman*

Germany, Munich, Alte Pinakothek, Albrecht Dürer, *Four Apostles*

Germany, Tiefenbronn, parish church, Lucas Moser, *Saint Mary-Magdalene Altarpiece*

Italy, Florence, Uffizi Galleries, Hugo van der Goes, *Portinari Altarpiece*

Italy, Palermo, Palazzo Abatellis, Antonello da Messina, *Virgin Annunciate*

Italy, Venice, Scuola di San Rocco, Jacopo Tintoretto, interior decoration

Spain, Madrid, Prado Museum, Hieronymus Bosch, *Garden of Earthly Delights*

Spain, Madrid, Prado Museum, Roger van der Weyden, *Descent from the Cross*

Switzerland, Geneva, Musée d'Art et d'Histoire, Konrad Witz, *Altarpiece of Saint Peter*

USA, New York, NY, Metropolitan Museum of Art, Robert Campin (Master of Flémalle), *Mérode Altarpiece*

19. Art and Renaissance Man

HIGH RENAISSANCE   LEONARDO DA VINCI   1452–1519

One of the most striking manifestations of the Renaissance is the multiplicity of the artists' talents. To name a few, Brunelleschi was a sculptor and architect-engineer who invented linear perspective; like Alberti, who was an architect and wrote ground-breaking treatises on art (*Della Pittura, De Statua, De Re Aedificatoria*) and astronomy and was also known as an athlete, a poet and a linguist. Michelangelo was a major poet in the Tuscan tongue, known as a sculptor who painted the most famous fresco ever, in the Sistine chapel, and as an architect built the greatest cupola ever, over the new Saint Peter's basilica in Rome. Raphael, at 35, was the Vatican's principal painter, a colossal job, but also the main architect of that largest ever church, Saint Peter, as well as the founder and superintendent of classical archeology (in Rome!). On top of that he was handsome and a charming personality, responsive to elegant ladies in Rome's jet-set, before he died at 37. His successor Jan van Scorel, less well-known (and possibly less charming), was a painter too, taking on his shoulders both the building of Saint Peter and the care of Rome's antiquities. In his homeland Holland, however, he had been an engineer of the waterworks his country was becoming famous for; an all-round man, we say, or better a Renaissance man. Leonardo da Vinci, to finish with him, was a painter, sculptor, and architect, but also an engineer, inventor of weaponry, learned philosopher and above all a surprising theoretical scientist in almost all known and unknown fields. Such diversity is more than human, from our point of view. Our point of view is wrong. Versatility was the rule in the older art world. Many of the artistic skills were technically related, all basically manual. The chief architect of a medieval cathedral had to be utterly skilled in most of the crafts concerned, from masonry to fresco and stained glass, and from sculpture to wood construction (for the roof), and not less skilled in calculus, accounting, diplomacy and some theology to crown it all. He could come from any of these disciplines. Giotto, the Gothic painter, built the bell tower of Florence cathedral and supervised the sculpture. So Pope Julius II could not expect nor accept his sculptor to *refuse* to also paint for him (Michelangelo swallowed his hot-blooded impertinence, of course).

If we distinguish these multiple talents among our Renaissance masters, it is that a beginning of specialization has set in, that will be typical of the coming centuries. The different techniques grow slowly apart, and a hierarchy of esteem comes into place. Be aware that this was not reassuring for the artists in question. Don't forget that they had a surprisingly low social status, whichever skill they practiced. Now they fought all for greater recognition. In the end painters and sculptors would succeed best; the workers in stained glass, mosaics, ceramics or tapestry, for example, would lose impact and become considered as minor artists.

Leonardo, in his way (unique here too!) makes us aware of a worrying situation. He travels on and on, moving from Florence to Milan and to Rome, and he dies in France. He accepts, if we may put it this way, any job. He would serve any master in any situation. There are so many competitors. His engineering skills are worth more than his painting and are rarer, so he mentions them first in his applications. From his notebooks we know, however, that he values painting most and in a famous comparison (*paragone*) tries to boast (or boost) it against sculpture (the opposite of Michelangelo's view). He claims painting is more civilized, refined, not as rudely manual. Painting, he would say, is a matter of the mind: *una cosa mentale.* (This sounds familiar to you if you read this book from the start). A very refined man himself, though very strong in his body, he likes to theorize about the arts when at work, formidable common sense reflections, but oftentimes takes almost more pleasure in the concept of a work than in its execution. The immaterial *idea* is the highest level or true goal of art, paradoxically. In his paintings he tries to render the immaterial concrete or the concrete immaterial. He calls it smoke, *sfumato,* the very air surrounding his models. It gives his figures both reality and unreal beauty. The balance sheet of Leonardo's performance is in consequence coherent but quite shocking: this great sculptor has left us no sculpture, and this great architect neither church nor palace; the best draughtsman of his age seems only to dialogue with his own brilliant mind in thousands of pages of inaccessible journals; and while his oil paintings can be counted on the fingers of two hands, his one famous fresco fell into ruin almost from the start and has never stopped to do so. With those few paintings and some handwritten private notebooks he achieved fame above all men: a pure legend, something of the mind, that is. As such he incarnates the European paradox in art between matter and non-matter.

The great artists, especially in Italy, climbing towards the aristocratic highlands between the feudal Middle Ages and the bourgeois New Times had no choice but be more than excellent in all the techniques they learned. They were the last generalists and the first specialists. Not the number but the quality of their skills must astonish us. Often in unknown perils, battling on all fronts like the last of the Mohicans, they opened the way to a new concept in art, *quality.* Their quality, according to their norms, will dominate all future art discussions and understanding.

In the 1960s, a very important art movement took place in America, Europe, and other continents, the name of which is Conceptual Art. It holds that the art is in the *concept* of it by the artist, and the execution is finally not essential but only a material exposition of it. A few names between many would include Joseph Kosuth, Lawrence Weiner, Michael Heizer and Daniel Buren. Its godfather would be Marcel Duchamp. Art goes from mind to mind, from artist to art appreciator; we don't really need its physical manifestation. The artist offers just a few indications in the form of objects or writings, so the idea can materialize if necessary. Those indications can, however, be as imposing as a mountain or discrete as a postcard. We are the first generation to understand this aspect of Leonardo's genius; maybe it is a hidden cause of his popularity. That sounds very noble, but the poignant irony is that our society has urged the artist back in the condition of a jack of all trades, a factotum or how would you call somebody who by everybody is expected to do everything in a project: from the first grandiose idea through its fatiguing and sometimes most humbling materialization, to transportation, public relation, selling, publication and threatening frustration. Without mentioning the modern artist's probable role of a modern parent of moderns kids. Compared to Leonardo, the contemporary artist risks to be rapidly on the way back to the Middle Ages. To say it nicely, the artist in our time has no choice but to be a universal artisan, a little Leonardo. Fortunately he or she doesn't often protest. He or she intuitively knows that art, like in the earliest times, comes from and goes to the entire human being, heart and hands, however primitive.

MAJOR WORKS AND MONUMENTS

France, Amboise, Le Clos Lucé

France, Château Chambord, Leonardo da Vinci (concept), *Monumental Staircase*

France, Paris, Centre Georges Pompidou, Musée National d'Art Moderne, Marcel Duchamp, *L.H.O.O.Q.* (on loan)

France, Paris, Musée du Louvre, Leonardo da Vinci, *Mona Lisa*

France, Paris, Musée du Louvre, Leonardo da Vinci, *Saint John the Baptist*

France, Paris, Musée du Louvre, Leonardo da Vinci, *Virgin and Child with St. Anne*

France, Paris, Place Royale, Daniel Buren, *Les Colonnes*

Great Britain, London, National Gallery, Leonardo da Vinci, *Virgin and Child with St. Anne and John the Baptist*

Great Britain, Windsor Castle, Royal Library, Leonardo da Vinci, *Notebooks*

Italy, Florence, Leon Battista Alberti, arch., church of Santa Maria Novella, *façade*

Italy, Milano, Convent of Santa Maria delle Grazie, Leonardo da Vinci, *Last Supper*

Italy, Rome, Vatican Museums, Papal Apartments, Raphael, *The School of Athens*

Italy, Rome, Vatican City, Basilica of St. Peter, Michelangelo, *Cupola*

Italy, Turin, Biblioteca Reale, Leonardo da Vinci, *Portrait of a Man in Red Chalk (Self-portrait?)*

Michelangelo Buonarroti, "Dante", "Joy May Kill" (poems)

Poland, Krakow, Wawel Castle, Czartoryski Museum, Leonardo da Vinci, *Lady with an Ermine*

Switzerland, Basel, Kunstmuseum, Jan van Scorel, *Portrait of the Anabaptist Leader David Joris*

USA, Silver Springs, NV, private collection, Michael Heizer, *#2/3 Displaced-Replaced Mass*

USA, Washington, D.C., National Gallery of Art, Leonardo da Vinci, *Ginevra de' Binci*

20. Art and the Nude

HIGH RENAISSANCE   **MICHELANGELO**   **1475–1564**

Nude is not the same as naked. They look similar but they mean the opposite. Nude is our mind, naked is our body. When Adam had sinned by eating from Eve's hand, he saw he was naked. He felt great shame. And he covered quickly his shameful parts with the help of their creator. This is the Hebrew view point. On the contrary, the Greek and Roman gods were uncovered from top to toe, proud to be nude. It was their ideal and privilege, like the best athletes in the arena. Western civilization comes from these opposite origins.

The Middle Ages had banned the body from the arts (not from common life). God and the saints were made of solemn draperies in few but significant colors. Apart from a face and hands, some-times feet, they had no flesh or bones; don't look for it even under their cloaks. No bodies, hence no nudity. Only Adam and Eve may show up naked once more, amidst the naked damned souls, burning in hell, there is nothing desirable about that. Their damnation, or punishment, was to lose their soul and to become a mere body. In the same spirit, the Virgin Mary was never preg-nant, or heavy, nor was she ever in labor or giving birth. There was an Annunciation and a Nativity, circumventing the physical reality of conception and birth. And Christ was not a baby, but God in the form of a little man, showing his little genitals as unde-niable proof of his manhood. The Circumcision (called the Pre-sentation in the Temple) was another proof of his human condi-tion. His nakedness on the cross resumed, indeed, the essence of his sacrifice.

Forget about the body (in art) until the Renaissance. Then you begin, moderately, to look for shoulders and breasts and hips and knees under the fabric, and musculature and reasonable proportions to carry those dignified cloaks of the saints. Anatomy becomes an issue, the relations between moving parts of the skeleton too, and the *contrapposto* found in Roman statues now openly admired by the cultural elite. The body takes form, still hidden in draperies, but standing in its own right.

The return (from ancient times) of the nude, however, was extremely slow. No doubt because art was essentially a public affair in a Christian society. After a surprising *Adam* and *Eve* by Jan van Eyck, another one by Masaccio, and a bronze *David* by Donatello, all around 1430, we have to wait till 1482 before Botticelli offers the *Birth of Venus*, the first female nude since antiquity, to a Medici patron. One understands better now the revolution and the shockwave caused by Michelangelo at the beginning of the next century. His marble *David*, over 14 feet high, a heroic nude as mighty as the best legendary Hellenistic examples stood on its pedestal not in a private courtyard, but in the middle of the central square of the almost largest city in Europe. This was not the artist's last statement. Soon after, from 1508-12 in Rome, Michelangelo painted the by far most gigantic painting ever tempted, on the ceiling of the pope's Sistine chapel. The pope was Julius II. In this fresco, representing the *Creation* according to the biblical *Genesis,* there are only bodies, and many of them are male nudes, many of them nude without a clear excuse, simply beautiful nudes. Beautiful? Horrible! Few understood the nude. The shock was too great. Many years later, between 1535 and 1541, when Paul III was pope, Michelangelo added an equally monumental *Last Judgment* to the decoration of the chapel. He went still one step further. The nudes were now Christ, Saint Peter, Saint Paul and the other apostles, without hid-ing anything. In the pope's own chapel! People were scandalized (and not before long *that* nudity was hidden by accidentally floating pieces of trompe-l'oeil cloth, which are still there).

All his life Michelangelo sculpted and painted nothing but human bodies. He knew about no other form to drape his pulsing expression. In one life-long stroke he put Western art in the face of its denied Greek and Roman origins. But he was the son of his age and didn't betray it; in his way, he was as medieval as Duccio or Dante. He sculpted and painted nothing but the spirit, in the best Western tradition, and in the best logic of art. In his hands the body became the beautiful drapery of the spirit. The visible part showing the invisible. The human body being the vessel of the divine, according to the story of the Creation and the Incarnation, this artist had no choice, no higher subject possible. The beauty of the body was destined to become the sense of art, its reason for being. It transformed the nude into an incomparable spiritual challenge, as its compelling beauty must become proportional to its divine status. Humankind has only the body to know the form of the soul. Better than drapery, the nude protected, or rather it symbolized the saints' innocence and virtue. Michelangelo defied here the most solemn Gothic stained glass.

Since the High Renaissance the nude is a strong theme in Western art. Not always deep and tortured, it always carries subtle sense; frivolous or profound, it always goes beyond the surface and touches the society where it is most sensitive or most vulnerable. During his life, Michelangelo has been able to see excellent examples of it, not all to his virile taste. The school of Venice, since long the rival in painting of Florence and Rome, started a subtle and sensual reading of the female nude, leaving behind the tragic or austere side that darkened the air around Michelangelo. Giorgione painted the first reclining *Venus* in a landscape. With it, the poetical tone is struck for good. Titian, nicknamed the painter of princes (or the prince of painters) picked up the theme, composing its most lyrical variations. His young admirer and competitor Veronese confirmed that the subject of the nude is an inexhaustible source of inspiration and from there we see that the history of European art is the history of its regard on the nude. Tintoretto, Rubens and Velázquez will carry on the torch for Venice, Flanders and Spain; Boucher, Fragonard and David for France in the eighteenth century; Goya, Courbet, Manet and Renoir for the beginning of the modern period; and Modigliani and Schiele, Mapplethorpe and Barthé for the twentieth century, again incomprehensive and scandalized. We could quote hundreds of other names in each time frame.

In art, one might say, the nude can never be naked.

MAJOR WORKS AND MONUMENTS

Austria, Vienna, Kunsthistorisches Museum, Tintoretto, *Susanna and the Elders*

France, Château de Chantilly, Raphael, *The Three Graces*

France, Paris, Musée d'Orsay, Edouard Manet, *Olympia*

France, Paris, Musée du Petit Palais, Gustave Courbet, *Le Sommeil* (« *Sleep* »)

Germany, Dresden, Gemäldegalerie Alte Meister, Giorgione, *Sleeping Venus*

Great Britain, London, National Gallery, Diego Velázquez, *Venus at her Mirror*

Great Britain, London National Gallery, Agnolo Bronzino, *Allegory with Venus and Cupid*

Italy, Florence, Museo dell'Accademia, Michelangelo, *David*

Italy, Florence, Museo Nazionale del Bargello, Donatello, *David*

Italy, Florence, Uffizi Galleries, Sandro Botticelli, *Birth of Venus*

Italy, Florence, Uffizi Galleries, Sandro Botticelli, *La Primavera* (« *Spring* »)

Italy, Florence, Uffizi Galleries, Titian, *Venus of Urbino*

Italy, Rome, Vatican Museums, Michelangelo, Sistine Chapel, *Creation* and *Last Judgment*

Italy, Rome, Vatican City, Basilica of St. Peter, Michelangelo, *Pietà*

Mapplethorpe, Robert, *"The Perfect Moment"* (1989 censured photo exhibit)

Spain, Madrid, Prado Museum, Francisco de Goya, *La Maja Desnuda*

Spain, Madrid, Prado Museum, Peter Paul Rubens, *The Three Graces*

USA, Hattiesburg, MS, University of Southern Mississippi, Richmond Barthé, *Africa Awakening*

USA, New York, NY, Metropolitan Museum of Art, Veronese, *Mars and Venus United by Love*

USA, Washington, D.C., National Gallery of Art, Titian, *Venus and Cupid with a Mirror*

21. Art and Reproduction

NEW FORMS IN THE NORTH   **DÜRER**   **1470–1528**

Around the middle of the millennium, in the years that saw the times tumble toward us, we see a growing awareness of the uniqueness of art objects and the rarity of great masters. At the same time we see the advent of its contrary: forgeries, copies, and multiplying techniques.

Fakes in the Middle Ages concerned not art but relics: a Vertebra of Saint Ursula, a Curl of the Holy Virgin, a Drop of Milk of the same, the Crown of Thorns. This last one cost France more than the construction of its shrine: the *Sainte Chapelle*. Their authenticity was not often contested, why should it: a Nail of the Holy Cross, a Tear of Saint Peter, a Head of Saint John? There were also many forged written documents: a letter from Emperor Constantine to the pope in Rome, a missive from the pope to a monastery, confirming some right or revenue. So few could read that it usually went unnoticed for centuries, the fakes looked soon as venerable as originals.

Copying was another question, it was honorable. Not much else was meant with "writing": copying venerated texts. In the arts it was almost prescribed: All *Madonna and Child* representations are supposed to be copies of Saint Luke's' original vision in the first century. But the copyists took all the freedom they thought necessary to enhance the message of the example. And not two *Madonna's* are identical. Every copy was unique. Uniqueness was not an issue. Everything was handmade and one of a kind in the Middle Ages. Every book or image, every bow or arrow, every nail or hammer, was unique. Then, around 1400, comes up the idea of the reproduction or, more exactly, multiple production of the same object. This object is an image. Do you realize the scope of the issue? Identical copies, for the first time! A revolution; not unlike the clone in our time, but with more offspring: these primitive woodcut prints were the first step on the way to mass production. In fact, Asian cultures had since long developed the technique of printing; we know brilliant samples from China, Korea, India, woodcuts for gigantic enterprises of prestigeous book printing, typically in small numbers though. It is possible Arab merchants brought "copies" to the Levant and that Venetian merchants introduced them in Europe. It can very well be invented a second time, too; it is not so difficult to imagine. The idea was already in the royal seal since thousands of years. More probable is the transmission from China to Europe of the art of making paper, an essential ingredient for the printing process. Until the end of the fourteenth century, Western Europe had written only on parchment or papyrus. Woodcuts would always lack the nobility of hand written and ornamented codices or papal bulls. It was exactly the key to their success. Simple and artless, paper was just good for them and, being inexpensive, the cuts became popular. And so they would generate two major cultural phenomena.

Texts first. Johannes Gutenberg, from Mainz in Germany, developed around 1450 the woodcut technology into the *industry* of printing by inventing metal moveable fonts. The lofty art of book making became a mechanical craft. Another German genius, the painter Albrecht Dürer from Nuremberg, did something similar the other way round; he turned the crude crafts of woodcut and engraving into an art.

One Dürer can exist in 20 or 40 copies. It seems a contradiction. Each one is an original, authenticated by the signature (the famous AD monogram) engraved on the block. To tell the truth, the artist has only made the model (a precise drawing) for a little team of woodcutters or copper engravers trained by him and doing a marvelous job of precision and sensibility. Who is in fact the artist, you wonder? You know it: the "inventor" of the model, the *cosa mentale,* not the manual craftsman. The output of the studio was considerable, and although the price of a print was relatively low, the number made it for the artist financially more interesting than painting. Paper and ink were cheaper than the pigments for paint. Human labor too. Dürer put enormous energy in producing great albums telling a long story in many good size prints: the *Passion of Christ,* the *Apocalypse.* He became famous and well-to-do, without the help of the Vatican or the Medici. He even conceived study books on perspective or anatomy for both students of art and art lovers.

Albrecht Dürer, the greatest painter of the German Renaissance, stands at the beginning of the new art form: printing. It is a difficult and demanding medium. Many artists have worked in it with great inventiveness; few have been able to express overwhelming talent. Just like in other techniques, the great successes come in waves limited in time and space. One such wave happened in Germany, coinciding more or less with Dürer's lifespan, going on to the middle of the sixteenth century. Lukas Cranach and Hans Baldung Grien are other great names here. A second wave occurs in Holland in the following century, the golden age. Rembrandt the etcher stands in the center, with Hercules Seghers and Adriaen van Ostade as wonderful second names. In the eighteenth century Francisco de Goya towers over all, something we can probably say too of Pablo Picasso in the twentieth century, though the modern age is particularly sensitive to printing techniques. Two lithographers of genius stand out in the nineteenth century: Honoré Daumier and Henri de Toulouse-Lautrec. At that time a wave like a tsunami rolled since a hundred years on the other side of the globe: over Japan. Rarely the harvest of an artistic movement has been richer than that of the Ukiyo-e, "pictures of the floating world." The subjects, printed in many colors from multiple blocks of cherry wood on handmade rice paper, go from portraits of actors and wrestlers, scenes from theatre and nightlife, to explicit erotic excitement and the peaceful beauty of national landscape during the Tokugawa shogunate. From this unparalleled outburst of creative energy, never equaled in terms of quantity, it is against all fairness to single out names at the expense of others. But would a chapter like this be complete without the names of Hokusai, Utamaro, or Hiroshige? Of Toyokuni, Kuniyoshi or Kunisada, the last one alone having produced over 20,000 designs for wood block prints, of which over 14,000 are catalogued so far? Like no other media these magnificent prints have opened western eyes to the spirit of the Far-East and no other art form from the Far-East had so great an influence on western art at a critical moment of its history.

Even more than the father of an art form, Albrecht Dürer is the ancestor of the graphic arts as a movement in modern civilization. He stands at the beginning of a line that leads via woodcut and engraving, etching, lithography, and wood-engraving, to photography, film, video, and finally the computer. Originally art media, apart from the last one, they are now the reproduction techniques in every household. Therefore it is interesting to link Dürer to another characteristic evolution in Europe, one he could not prevent to arise in the art world: the growing appreciation of the *unique* piece. And when the artists were not asking for it, since they stood at the head of a workshop, the society imposed it on them. Artists would become the guardian angels of a medieval concept of hand-made uniqueness, a concept today more vigorous than ever. Its rise was certainly related to growing attachment to the idea of uniqueness of the human being. In art we speak about the original: we collect them.

Like churches in the Middle Ages had collected relics, monasteries books, and kings all kind of curiosities, from nature and from human craft, after 1500 we see the coming of age of the art collectors. Princes and bishops, soon bankers and warlords, then merchants, and even poets would go further than the traditional commission of a chapel decoration, an altar piece or a portrait from an artist. Rather than for a question of public display, they would buy a painting or a print for the personal love of the artist, for his or her name, reputation and commercial value. They would give money even for a drawing, a study that in earlier times would not have survived the completion of a final work. The private art collection was born. With time the hand of the master (the *signature*) became far more valuable than any imaginable subject matter or even the material. And while the reputation of the masters rose, the number of their *"authentic"* pieces to obtain would diminish. Their prices would go up. Copies would appear or fakes. It generated veneration for the original to a degree that hitherto was reserved for religious or family objects; here started an evolution that has not stopped in our days, as everyone knows.

This evolution was slow. For a long time a good handmade copy was almost worth an original. Artists would make copies themselves or have them made by apprentices. They would develop the graphic media to have their images reproduced (and protect their copyright!). It took centuries before the cult of the original reached the almost frightful dimensions it has now. A proclaimed Leonardo drawing, recently on the market (2010), if authenticated, would be worth the annual salary of some 10,000 workers (in America!). If the same drawing proved to be the German romantic piece that other experts believe it is, three of those workers could purchase it in a few months.

Leonardo is dead and universally recognized, which explains in part his value on the market. But the combined development of art history and the art market have drawn living artists since the end of the nineteenth century in the same orbit. Originality became a goal in itself as a marker of style and personality, often spiraling into the spectacular, the performance and mass entertainment. The market bought it, for spectacular prices, entertaining the masses. Pointing at the risk of perversion of the system, some artists protested. In 1964 Lucio Fontana made little cans of *"artist shit"*. The market bought it, too; you can admire the originals in prestigious galleries. Handsome, in fact.

One is not surprised that since the beginning, this blinding veneration of the masters has been at the origin of a real army of forgers. Only art history and art science can stop them, but for now they discover that the number of forgers is growing every day. They accompany the arts like lackeys the king: flattering and false, hollow and harmful.

Well, let us be fair: they don't do just harm. Like none, they sharpen our mind.

MAJOR WORKS AND MONUMENTS

Brueghel, Pieter the Elder, *Big Fish Eat Little Fish* (engraving)

Cock, Hieronymus, *Aux Quatre Vents* (publishing house in Antwerp)

Colonna, Francesco, *Hypnerotomachia Poliphili* (woodcuts)

Cranach, Lucas the Elder, *Adam and Eve* (woodcut)

Cranach, Lucas the Elder, *Portrait of Martin Luther* (engraving)

Dürer, Albrecht, *Knight, Death and Devil* (engraving)

Dürer, Albrecht, *Melancholia* (engraving)

Dürer, Albrecht, *The Triumph of Maximilian of Austria* (woodcut)

Grien, Hans Baldung, *Witches' Sabbath* (chiaroscuro woodcut)

Holbein, Hans the Younger, *Dance of Death* (woodcuts)

Hiroshige, Utagawa, *53 Stations of the Tokaido* (woodblock prints)

Hokusai, Katsushika, *36 Views of Mount Fuji* (woodblock prints)
Leyden, Lucas van, *Milk Maid and Farm Hand* (engraving)
Pollaiuolo, Antonio del, *Battle of the Ten Nude Men* (engraving)
Raimondi, Marcantonio, *The Last Supper after Raphael* (engraving)
Rembrandt (van Rijn), *The Hundred Guilder Print* (etching)

Schongauer, Martin, *The Temptation of Saint Anthony* (engraving)
Seghers, Hercules, *Landscape with Fir* (etching on painted paper)
USA, Malibu, CA, J. Paul Getty Museum, *Getty Kouros* (fake)
Wolgemut, Michael, *The Nuremberg Chronicles* (woodcuts)

22. Art and Popular Culture

NEW FORMS IN THE NORTH   **BRUEGHEL**   **1525 – 68**

As a sensitive person in our twenty-first century you must wonder how after twenty-one lessons about the arts the topic of the
common people and their life has never surfaced. Remember how
political and social institutions recuperate the power of the arts
at their advantage. People of the lower classes should caress no
illusions. But even rarely visible, they are not absent. During the
sixteenth century, their reality seemed to jump onto the stage,
North of the Alps with more conviction than South of them.

The Italian Renaissance reinforced old elites and established new
ones. The ideal of antiquity was an aristocratic one, and the Catholic Church welcomed the pagan heritage as a means to fortify its
positions of authority that had weakened toward the end of the
Middle Ages. It would result in what in religious history is called
the Counter-Reformation. The ideal (and mission) of art and beauty
for the Renaissance and the Baroque (*i.e.* 1450 – 1800) translated into *unity, hierarchy* and *majesty*. It was expressed through
mythological, historical and, above all, biblical themes. This ideal
crossed the Alps, but not without alterations. The Flemish and
the Dutch, the Germans and the English, the Czech and the Swiss,
to name the more prominent ones, challenged that theological
unity of Church, Nobility and Kingdoms. They fought centralization and hierarchy and they mistrusted majesty. It was said that
they couldn't understand; possibly so. They clearly didn't want to.
They protested with all means, moved by a spirit of independence
and individual morality. The Reformation presented itself as the
religious foundation of it. Protestants defended old fashioned

values and threatened privileges, small scale government and the autonomy of the family. Many mistrusted art straightforwardly. In the process they discovered a more humble beauty, or the beauty of more humble things. Transferred to painting it meant, with some exaggeration: landscape and seascape instead of the Olympic gods, still-life and flowers instead of Madonna's, portraits of burghers and salesmen, instead of kings and bishops. Non-religious painting became possible, necessary even. The sacred nature of art started to move out of the church, into lay society.

One is tempted to say Southern Europe in its art, especially in the schools of Florence, Rome and Venice, followed later by France and Spain, would favor the ideal and the past, Northern Europe the real and the present. This view of the matter would be too schematic, though; the parting of the ways, undeniable, was slow and never complete. Flanders occupied a position in the middle, and Antwerp was its center. In the seventeenth century, the all-embracing genius of Rubens would throw the bridge between North and South. In the sixteenth century it had been a Fleming in the same city of Antwerp, who had shown with astounding energy the abyss between them and had elevated northern art to its own heights.

The name of the artist who exemplified the extraordinary breakthrough was Pieter Brueghel. While the Italian Renaissance artists had given life to history and archeology, Brueghel has done the same for anthropology and sociology, of which he can be seen as a forerunner. He became the sharpest observer of the life and customs of the common people in his country and his age. In paintings and widely distributed prints he depicted peasants and villagers, beggars and soldiers, pilgrims and priests, opening our eyes to the most common behavior with a passion until then reserved for the hallowed or venerable. In doing so and thanks to a very lively though precise brush, he stages the most comic cartoon if it were not that he conveys at the same time the highest moral commitment. He is able to make us indulge in the extravaganza of a rural *Wedding Dance*, to study the local folklore of *Carnival and Lent,* to pity *Begging Cripples* as well as captive *Monkeys,* and to enjoy from our comfortable armchair the Netherlandish winter habit of *Skating on a Frozen Canal.* All aspects of daily life receive his most sincere interest, intelligent judgment and meticulous treatment in paint.

Pieter Brueghel, named the Elder, because he was the father and grandfather of artists with the same name, was even more the godfather of several art genres soon to become universal: landscape, daily life of the more modest classes, disaster of warfare, and even caricature. He must have been a learned man, a humanist friend of humanists, a traveler, and a reader of books. However, he transposes his knowledge without a shade of pretension or moralizing. We can't help to hear his laugh, to admire his compassion. Everybody can enjoy his theatre, without questioning, without even remarking the innumerable subtle symbols that enrich the presentation for the learned folks. His pictorial skill is such that the humblest subject, a *Kermis (Vi-llage Fair)*, a *Harvest* scene or a *Peasant Wedding Feast,* achieves in his hands the dignity of the greatest events in world history. And we smile thinking about the power and the diversity of art. What Michelangelo did for the nude, *i.e.* discover its *soul,* his contemporary Pieter Brueghel did for the peasant and the poor, the simple of the mind, the anonymous crowd. He makes them laugh and he makes them weep, he makes them fight and kiss and eat and drink and smoke; he doesn't make them pretty or polite, but he places the humble and the hungry in the center of humanity.

His *Birth of Christ* takes place in a village of his country, and Mary is a peasant girl. His *Massacre of the Innocents* (by the soldiers of King Herod, a Christmas story) becomes a raid on a village by the Spanish mounted police, Flanders being under the control of (Catholic) Spain. Here the symbols are evident, which is not always the case with more peaceful scenes. The greater art's resemblance with reality, the more symbolic it must become. Art reaches out beyond the actual artwork.

The paintings and engravings by Brueghel the Elder introduce us into the culture of the people, as it was written in no book and would have been lost without him. Not only its traditional wisdom that he laid down in the absurd village of the *Proverbs,* an even more exceptional painting leads us into a town where only children are; they play with the serious tranquility of grown-ups their hundreds of *Children's Games.* And with the children and the fools, the blind and the dumb, the fat and the lean, the servants and the sick and all the others as real as we are, humor enters into art, the great liberating laugh that makes life livable for us all and even well worth to be lived.

It is difficult to exaggerate the width of Brueghel's spiritual heritage. In literature we dare think of Cervantes, Molière, Mark Twain, Charlie Chaplin and John Steinbeck. In painting we must name the seventeenth century schools of Holland and Flanders. Think of him too in relation to Goya in Spain, to Realism in France and in the twentieth century to Regionalism and realistic photography in America, recording the suffering from the Great Depression.

MAJOR WORKS AND MONUMENTS

Austria, Vienna, Kunsthistorisches Museum, Pieter Brueghel the Elder, *Battle Between Carnival and Lent*

Austria, Vienna, Kunsthistorisches Museum, Pieter Brueghel the Elder, *Children's Games*

Belgium, Antwerp, Museum Mayer van den Bergh, Pieter Brueghel the Elder, *Dulle Griet*

Belgium, Brussels, Musées Royaux des Beaux-Arts, Pieter Aertsen, *Cook in Front of the Stove*

Belgium, Ghent, Museum voor Schone Kunsten, Pieter Brueghel the Younger, *Village Lawyer*

Evans, Walker, *Bud Fields, Cotton Sharecropper* (photograph)

France, Paris, Musée du Louvre, Louis and Matthieu Le Nain, *Peasant Family*

Germany, Berlin, Gemäldegalerie, Frans Hals, *Malle Babbe*

Germany, Frankfurt, Städel Museum, Adriaen Brouwer, *The Bitter Draught*

Great Britain, London, National Gallery, Quentin Matsys, *The Ugly Duchess*

Italy, Milan, Pinacoteca Ambrosiano, Jan Brueghel the Elder, *Grand Bouquet in a Vase*

Netherlands, Amsterdam, Rijksmuseum, Adriaen van Ostade, *Peasants Drinking and Dancing in a Barn*

Netherlands, Amsterdam, Rijksmuseum, Jan Steen, *Soo d'Ouden Songen Piepen de Jonghen*

Netherlands, The Hague, Museum Mauritshuis, Joachim Beuckelaer, *Kitchen scene with disciples at Emmaus*

Netherlands, The Hague, Museum Mauritshuis, Jan Vermeer, *Girl with a Pearl Earring*

Russia, St. Petersburg, Hermitage Museum, Bartolome Esteban Murillo, *Boy with a Dog*

USA, Chicago, IL, Art Institute, Grant Wood, *American Gothic*

USA, New York, NY, Metropolitan Museum of Art, Pieter Brueghel the Elder, *Wheat Harvest*

23. **Art and Illusion 2**
  (Light)

BAROQUE   VELAZQUEZ - VERMEER   17ᵀᴴ - 18ᵀᴴ CENTURIES

As far as the arts and letters are concerned, the seventeenth century presents a summit in European civilization. And don't think of William Shakespeare and John Milton alone, or of Inigo Jones and Sir Christopher Wren: there was also *Le Grand Siècle* for France and a *Golden Age* for Spain, Holland, Flanders and Italy. Remember, to concentrate on the visual arts, Caravaggio and Bernini (and Annibale Carracci!), Rubens and Van Dyck (and Jacob Jordaens!), Rembrandt and Vermeer (and Frans Hals!), El Greco and Velázquez (and Francisco de Zurbarán!), De la Tour and Poussin (and "Claude" Lorrain!). Everybody knows these names, and they are only the tip of the iceberg. Significantly, these randomly (or traditionally) chosen names are all of painters, except for Bernini, one sculptor. Painting had, with theatre, become the stage of the European spirit. Architects followed immediately and they would, for two hundred years, all over the continent, forge the most dramatic and astonishing decors in stone and stucco. A few examples: Bernini and Borromini in Rome, Guarini et Juvarra in Turin, Dientzenhofer and Pöppelmann in Prague and Dresden, Fischer von Erlach in Vienna, Dominikus Zimmermann in Bavaria. Mentioning the stage, painting saw itself often as theatre, reduced to two dimensions. An illusion of theatre. If you recognize that theatre is itself a play of illusions, you see how much of illusion we need to approach the truth. It is what all those famous artists had understood in common. They left us all masterpieces in this vein. Their technical skills had grown so refined that the *trompe-l'oeil* was taken for granted. It is usually taken for granted by us, too; without questioning, we accept it as the normal condition for painting. And the better works the magic!

These masters of illusion lorded over perspective, knowing that the less was shown, the more the eye of the public would do the work. Their success was principally based on their painterly (and masterly) handling of light, so much so, that in art history books that has become the ultimate criterion for greatness or genius. Very serious and dry art historians have become lyrical when it came to this subject (helped by a dose of national chauvinism). Light has many facets and as many ways to be painted, of course, and it won't help us either to compare great artists as horses in a race. The ones mentioned above were all very different, in personality, background and goals. They have all added their part to our understanding and enjoying the mystery of light. God's first word in the Jewish creation story, light is both the physical and the symbolical principle of existence. What the masters of the Byzantine Empire had done with mosaic, and the Gothic centuries with stained glass, the painters of the Baroque tried with oil: enlighten the obscurity of the material world. Caravaggio, first in the Baroque line, sent his sudden rays into the dark of the Roman underworld; we call it *chiaroscuro.* El Greco, from Crete, made his light reverberate in Castilian Toledo as if reflecting on immaterial mosaics or trembling Venetian canals with distorting mystic effects. Vermeer captured the light of his country filtered by the high windows of its homes and solidified it like milk, lying over middle-class habits a cloak of almost sacred silence. Replace milk by silk and you have the difference between Holland and Spain, or between Vermeer and Velázquez (or burghers and kings!).

Diego Velázquez is particularly daring when he applies these seventeenth century flashes of insight to royal portraits. His goal as the court artist of the king of Spain is to show the ruler as a superior human being. His talent as painter is to show that painting is the superior art. Not only superior to sculpture and tapestry, but if possible to philosophy. Therefore in one image, apparently innocent, in fact sharp as a riddle as can only invent a superior painter, our world is shown to be pure illusion; but this illusion is elevated by his art to an apparition of sublime intelligence. In *Las Meninas* he paints the theatre of an improvised and imaginary portrait session of the royal couple. He stages an all-convincing three-dimensional space, a really existing room in the palace, its walls covered with paintings. But the king and queen are missing; to our relief by the way, the etiquette of the court is painfully exacting. We wouldn't even be allowed in here as observers. Thus, what we expected, we don't see. What we see, we didn't expect: a surprisingly chaotic and noisy scene with the disarming little *Infanta,* and maids of honor (*meninas)* and jesters and dogs and servants and what not, yes! a painter and the back of a canvas. We see them in silver light, falling through an unknown window behind us into the dark palace room just right to wrap around the princess, leaving all others in shades and darkness. Impossible to paint with this light, but the painter in front of his huge canvas shows no fear. We would like to know what he painted yet. His eye darts in our direction; looks right through us; don't we exist, in fact? What does he see? And what the little Margarita? With a shock we become aware of our error: the royal portrait we didn't pay attention to at the far end of the room is not a portrait at all, but a mirror, and it mirrors the royalty who must be *in pose* for the painter quite exactly where we are (if we were not an illusion). We, the subjects, cannot ever see the king of flesh and blood; we can only contemplate his image, made of reflected light. The king we may see is made of light; like *divine*. The illusion becomes a vision.

If this were not enough, Velázquez's painting style is marvelously adapted to this evasive approach of reality. He models not forms but dots of light: no drawing, no outline, no sculpted body or cut out dress, nothing fixed, all there is is but a spray of drops of paint, which evoke all the tones of gray that the eye can distinguish between light and dark and suffice to reveal this world. The forms are not on the canvas but in our mind. Our eye and brain build up a reality from what is nothing but a floating illusion.

The *Las Meninas* group portrait, *the* emblematic work of Spanish art, was painted in 1656 and originally called *The Family.* The royal family, that is. King Philip IV was never described by history as a very successful ruler. A few years before the unique *Family Portrait* was done, in 1648, he had lost one of his crown jewels, Holland, bitterly regretted, after not less than eighty years of war. But he was a fine connoisseur of art, and he appointed Diego Velázquez as his court artist, a stroke of genius. For the young man it was a great honor and at the same time a golden cage. He was supposed to do portraits of the royal family and close entourage, and that was about it. His real honor is to have not lost his intrinsic inspiration at this deeply Catholic, archaistic, overly aristocratic, conservative court with its notorious etiquette and boring discipline, living in old palaces and cold castles for forty years. How different life was in Amsterdam, Holland: no king, no court, no church, no manners (as they would say in Spain), but merchants and craftsmen from all over the world and heretic preachers in new churches and liberal professors in new schools, and mansions and warehouses arising all over the fast growing city. No fixed job here for any painter, competition was the rule, with its exciting opportunities and its terrible risks. Every painting had to be sold to keep the workshop open. Isn't it striking, seen the contrasting circumstances, that *the* emblematic work of Dutch art is also a monumental group portrait, this one made a few years *before* the peace treaty mentioned above. It also goes by a nickname, *The Night Watch,* it was painted by Rembrandt. Isn't it striking that the key of its dramatic success, here too, is the painter's ability to play with the illusions of space, movement, even sound and smell? Realized by a savvy play with light! Rembrandt uses indeed all the props and tricks of the theatre on his stage, including the lighting. The sitters who commissioned the portrait don't sit and don't look like they look in daily life; they perform an act in a festive parade, according to their grade in a pseudo military officer's club, a highly social and artificial act, every one of these burghers showing up in his most magnificent, almost aristocratic attire. The signal of departure is given and there they walk out, from chaos to order, from obscurity to the light. All is theatrical here, and therefore it looks so real, no doubt. It worked even better in the painting's original situation, as it was hanging in a shadowy corner lit by high windows on one side. Rembrandt was famous for his efficient handling of light and dark. He demonstrates it with sensibility and intelligence, bravely building his entire composition on the distribution of just that: dramatic *chiaroscuro* is his forte. Soon we don't see paint anymore, only modulations of colors in full light or deep shade. He highlights one face after another, suggesting the interpersonal dynamics of the group, depth and width and suspense, giving a chance here to psychology, there to rank, costume, function or relationships. In short, the result of these fireworks of artificiality is an almost haunting feeling of reality. As the people in his own time said and we experience it again in the museum, the *Night Watch* is alive and condemns all the others to being only paintings. Playing cards, they said, in fact. And from an ordinary realistic portrait session we walk out with the conviction of having experienced a mystery.

The special fascination of the described works lies in the fact that here an action is suddenly frozen in time. The illusion of life comes from its treatment as a "still", which word is now used in film but originally means *dead*. We keep our breath and seem to wait when the interrupted movement will be free again to go on. It is the common denominator of the "breathtaking" works of the time, left in Italy and Flanders in numberless churches, in London, Paris, Madrid and Amsterdam in palaces and mansions, and in Austria, Bavaria, Scandinavia, Russia and more until the end of the eighteenth century. Movement is the attribute of life. Stillness is the attribute of objects. Now objects have their place in painting too. They appear when the painter needs to set a contrast with the live actors and drape a lofty history with some humble reality: hanging curtains, a carpet on a table, a statue, a plate, a knife, some dispersed fruits, a flower in a vase. Our attitude is different. We don't hold our breath but take our time to observe and meditate. Are these objects painted as they really are? We become very critical. We believe we can judge freely. Someone who can paint an apple well, said Caravaggio, can paint a figure, and he painted a basket full of them, as captivating as his *David Beheading Goliath*. Now the epoch reserved a specialized approach to object paintings, calling them by the name of still life. The public's demand of reality was and is here greater than ever. The level of illusion heightens. The treatment of perspective and light can only satisfy us if it renders reality perfectly and ... make us forget the humble status of the still object compared to the active human. Still life was a great success. The lively, even stormy Baroque spirit needed its moments of rest. In this exercise of immobility, it was again the Spanish and Dutch schools that excelled. They would answer as well to monastic silence in Spain as to burgher tranquility in Holland. The first would pursue ascetic simplicity, the latter the balanced exhibition of the riches in a society discovering opulence. Their (artistic) achievement was such that still life would become a rival of history painting with the public. It still is.

And still life is still associated in the public's mind to Dutch painting. Justly so. In Holland this genre was overwhelming in quantity as well as quality. Many sub-genres developed, of which flower painting became beloved in the whole world. In fact, the famous Dutch home interiors could be considered as such a sub-genre of still life. Though people appear in them, they are anonymous, nameless mothers and children, happy pipe smokers, women in a kitchen or at their toilette, looking at themselves in a mirror, trying a necklace or writing a letter to a friend, believing they are unobserved. One moment they don't move, and that is the moment the painter chooses for eternity. These paintings are simple, their sole value and soul hides in the faultless presentation of a reality we pretend we can all judge, because it seems to be ours. Of course this is an illusion, never mind. Jan Vermeer knew. He knew how the human sense of reality depended on the perception of light. The perfect illusion. And that is what he painted. Not much more than that. So well that his silent stories of light move us to the core. Every time we see them again.

MAJOR WORKS AND MONUMENTS

Belgium, Antwerp, Cathedral of Our Lady, Peter Paul Rubens, *Descent of the Cross*

France, Rennes, Musée des Beaux-Arts, Georges De La Tour, *The New-Born*

Germany, Dresden, Gemäldegalerie Alte Meister, Jacob van Ruisdael, *Rainbow over the Jewish Cemetery*

Germany, Frankfurt, Städel Museum, Nicolas Poussin, *Storm in a Landscape with Pyramus and Thisbe*

Great Britain, London, Royal Collection, St. James's Palace, Jan Vermeer, *The Music Lesson*

Italy, Genoa, Palazzo Rosso, Anthony van Dyck, *Equestrian Portrait of Anton Giulio Brignole-Sale*

Italy, Milan, Biblioteca Ambrosiana, Caravaggio, *Basket of Fruit*

Italy, Rome, Church of San Luigi dei Francesi, Caravaggio, *The Calling of Saint Matthew*

Italy, Rome, Church of Santa Maria della Vittoria, Gian Lorenzo Bernini, *The Ecstasy of Saint Teresa di Avila*

Italy, Rome, Museo e Galleria Borghese, Gian Lorenzo Bernini, *Apollo and Daphne*

Netherlands, Amsterdam, Rijksmuseum, Rembrandt, *The Jewish Bride*

Netherlands, Amsterdam, Rijksmuseum, Rembrandt, *The Night Watch (The Militia Company of Frans Banning Cocq and Willem van Ruytenburgh)*

Netherlands, Haarlem, Frans Halsmuseum, Willem Claesz. Heda, *Still life with Pie, Ewer and Crab*

Spain, Madrid, Prado Museum, Peter Paul Rubens, *Equestrian Portrait of the Duke of Lerma*

Spain, Madrid, Prado Museum, Diego Velázquez, *Las Meninas (A Portrait of the Royal Family)*

Spain, Madrid, Prado Museum, Diego Velázquez, *Rendition of Breda*

Spain, Madrid, Prado Museum, Francisco de Zurbarán, *Still life with Pottery Jars*

Spain, Toledo, Church of Santo Tomé, El Greco, *Burial of the Count of Orgaz*

USA, Detroit, MI, Institute of Arts, Rachel Ruysch, *Flowers in a Glass Vase*

USA, New York, NY, Metropolitan Museum of Art, El Greco, *View of Toledo*

USA, New York, NY, Frick Collection, Jan Vermeer, *Lady with her Maidservant Holding a Letter*

24. **Art and the Self**

BAROQUE **REMBRANDT** **1606 - 69**

In the beginning of the seventeenth century, in the modest city of Leiden, Holland, the young Rembrandt started a project that would occupy him all his life. It was new and it would be a rare, if not unique project for centuries. He painted (and etched) himself during almost half a century, his whole career. For him, in the beginning, it was not a major concern, which was to portray wealthy burghers and to conceive great compositions of biblical and historical events. He did well, moved to Amsterdam and was honored in the fast-growing city.

Amsterdam was something of a phenomenon: from a modest town of fishermen it grew in a few decades to be the center of world trade. Its rather tolerant administration attracted people from all over Europe in great numbers, often political or religious exiles, but also legions of artists, like Rembrandt. He was ambitious, competitive, competent and a successful teacher. His manner, although steeped in the best traditions, was soon recognized as original and personal, functioning like a trademark. In this city of bustling business, he was just another businessman. He didn't refuse the title, but aware of his genius, he must have reserved moments of reflection about the nature of his special trade: art. Art, he knew, was not only a question of doing, but of thinking. A self-portrait was the outcome of such contemplation on the status of the artist.

It was the golden age of portraiture. The previous chapter gave attention to some imperial masterworks and their masters, so let's make room for a few others. Because how not to mention here the civic militia groups by Frans Hals, now in the precious museum of Haarlem? Or his *Laughing Cavalier* in the vast London Wallace Collection? Like this quite forgettable lad was raised by Hals to an unforgettable icon of young male martial bearing, numberless characters are forever engraved in our memories as a moving catalog of mankind's diversity. The Fleming Anthony van Dyck is almost alone responsible for our image of the English aristocracy during two hundred years, like his teacher Rubens had done before him for the Genoa noblemen and women. Spain meant more than the court alone and Zurbarán and Murillo have left us noble images of the monks and the lower classes. Philippe de Champaigne would already be famous if he had done nothing but the portraits of Richelieu, as later Hyacinthe Rigaud only for his images of Louis, the Sun-King. All of these could be called the spiritual children of sixteenth-century Raphael, Bronzino, Titian and Tintoretto, and of course Italy continued to produce excellent portraits in the new century. Think only of the Cardinals and Popes by Reni and Guercino. We admire these artists, hired to flatter quite bluntly the social status of their patrons, for their inexhaustible capacity to frankly reveal a personality, analyze a character, read thoughts, and mirror a soul.

In less than two centuries the portrait had thus become the dominating commission in art. Self-portraits developed, with reason, as a marginal by-product, but we moderns are partial to them. Since the Early Renaissance we find them as a form of signature in major compositions, a face cunningly hidden in the crowd, the only one to watch us with intensity. Jan van Eyck signed the first single panel self-portrait, 1433, but we have to wait until 1500, when Dürer picked up the idea and made it into a slowly developing custom for painters. For quite a few northern sixteenth-century artists, women between them (!), we are as happy to know how they saw themselves. In Italy we recognize Raphael in his youth and Titian in his old age (Rembrandt's prime examples) and ardent Tintoretto. In the seventeenth century, collectors confirm the existence of a minor genre: the king of England, Charles I, and the brother of the Duke of Tuscany, Cardinal Leopoldo de Medici started to collect them systematically. They commissioned them or received them from artists who expected a favor. The noble Rubens, distant Poussin, poetic Van Dyck, romantic Salvator Rosa, the loving sister Rosalba Carriera, we know their face from two, four, sometimes six or eight convincing pieces. Exactly as they wish us to remember them. They show gravity (the attitude of the thinker), a certain pride (a distinction received from the king, for instance), little ostentation, no underscoring of their manual craft either, sometimes even ignoring that fact. Psychological truth? No doubt, but the century would have preferred the idea of *moral* truth, or (social) *virtue*. They continued to like allegorical associations with historical events or philosophical personifications. Two strong opposites as examples: Caravaggio, humiliated, showed his traits as the face of decapitated Goliath in the victorious hand of young David! The giant artist killed by his uncontrolled pride. Artemisia Gentileschi painted herself with brushes in hand, painting actually, the pride of her craft. The composition was original, the idea traditional, appropriate and very daring: because she was a woman, and she claimed to be the allegory of painting herself.

Now Rembrandt. He is definitely a case apart. We know some 65 self-portraits, without mentioning the many fakes (think about this: a fake self-portrait), produced in a steady rhythm of one or two per year. Sometimes he used his own figure in a historical composition (*The Prodigal Son,* with Saskia, his wife, as the prostitute! Now in Dresden), or disguised in rich clothes, posing with a poodle, as a soldier, grimacing, handsome, thoughtful, sometimes tired like the apostle Paul, or laughing like the philosopher Democritus. In the most powerful ones, towards the end of his life, he is the painter, tools in hand, very dignified, very pensive, silent, grandiose even. And sometimes he's just himself. Is that possible? No. He stills wears his flat beret, identifying him as a professional painter in his time, as Rembrandt for us.

This is a splendid autobiography in paint. We realize that nothing calls upon us as strongly as a human face, and behind the face a life. We see a man grow from young to old, a moving story, four centuries old and as young as we are. Rembrandt has done something that speaks powerfully to us moderns: he stands out of the crowd. Powerful but risky. Spectators have massively identified with him: fascinated by the biographical side of art and artist, they searched for *and* recognized his traits in every sort of painting or drawing. Wishful art appreciation. And after having exhausted this goldmine to get close to the man, they looked for his mother, his father, his brother, and they found them, his wife, his concubines, his children. This fired the imagination. Many legends have been woven around him, in the form of history or novels (and films!). The stories changed with their writers, they changed with the times, with the countries, with the talents, and the intentions, drastically. They were never the story Rembrandt told. The historic painter disappeared behind the fiction. As long as we are aware of it, it's not a problem; but are we aware?

This is the intriguing problem of portraiture: do we look at the painter or at his model? Especially intriguing when the model is the painter!

Rembrandt seems to paint self-portraits to meditate. He invites the spectator, like in older times before an icon, to meditate with him. About truth, illusion, reality, history, religion, social rank, virtue, family, love, life, and so on. In one word about art, he's an artist. He approaches these themes each time from another angle. But each time the whole man is there, made of many facets in one image, none of which we can isolate. With time the central theme defines itself more clearly: is the essence of a man in his physical being? In his flesh and his dress, his profession and his success? The answer of the self-portraits is yes and no. *Yes*, when they show a man growing from young to old, from smooth skin to wrinkles, from blond hair to grey, what else is life? It is interesting to watch, and to paint, though possibly hard to live. There is the coming and the going of riches, the attractive triviality of social status, the rise and fall of the body. Is life but a series of anecdotes, filed as Rembrandt van Rijn, whom everybody knows? *No*, there is more to say, though, because this row of faces and garb shows something else, difficult to define: a unique being, which stays with the painter from the beginning to the end. The visible face speaks about an invisible other behind the mask of flesh, one that is constantly gaining in eloquence and presence. The painter tries to unveil it. And discovers he's not that good in it. He fails: he paints the mask he wants to take away. He gets closer though. He has to try again, try to paint the mask away. To see beyond the anecdote. Behind the surface is Rembrandt him *self*. And Rembrandt is the artist to give that self a mirror. He links it to the face.

Maybe he found that the self, finally, is the artist.

When the painter thinks about himself in painting, he thinks about art. Not psychology.

In a self-portrait he paints himself twice in one: his "person," *and* his person done in his "style." *Only he* can paint himself in his own style. His "person" resembles him. But his style *is* him; it is his real self-portrait. This style is his in every one of his works. Every one of his works is a self-portrait.

The answer to the question "Who is Rembrandt?" is "His art-works!"

Since Rembrandt every artwork is a portrait of the artist. The artist is in every work, in every gesture, in every brushstroke.

Every art work a brush stroke of the self.

You know this unconsciously. When you see a painting, you say: Look! Cézanne, or look! Dali, even if what you see is an apple, or the strangest long-legged elephant.

That is also why you hate the forgers, however great their skill. They belie the self, they belie the law, of art, and sometimes we are able to put them into jail.

In the nineteenth century, psychology became the new science and replaced morality in the study of human behavior. The "self", this heritage from the confrontation of the Reformation and the Counter-Reformation, received its scientific definition and contours. Rembrandt gained in esteem in the public's eye and pushed Raphael and Rubens from the highest podium of universal glory. Modern man is in search for the self, and great is the artist who shows the way. Goya was the first one to realize Rembrandt's quest. The self-portrait knew an acute popularity from 1850 on. Very consistent artists in the field were Gustave Courbet, Vincent van Gogh, Paul Gauguin, Egon Schiele, Paula Modersohn-Becker, Frida Kahlo, Andy Warhol. Under the influence of Sigmund Freud's writings, Surrealism made us aware of the inescapable presence of the artist in his or her art. Salvador Dali hid many distorted portraits of his nose and eyelashes in the most improbable places. Joan Miró wrote his own name over and over, as a modern calligraphy, without almost anybody recognizing it. And Picasso's signature earned market value without even being attached to a work: There was his self. When he paid by check, people would keep the piece of paper with his signature, rather than bank the money. This is what Marcel Duchamp had foreseen and responded to when he exposed his first *Ready Made.* These are found objects, a bicycle wheel or a bottle rack, shown without intervention of the artist on the object, apart from the label. Then he stopped making art at all, preferring to play chess. But the public didn't let him escape, whatever he did. He became himself his artwork. Art might be dead but the artist was vividly alive: the extreme concept, the ultimate paradox. Hyper-sensitive Salvador Dali understood this very well, in conceiving his own tragic-comic art clown for an ambulant self-portrait. Andy Warhol drew the conclusions for the future.

MAJOR WORKS AND MONUMENTS

Austria, Vienna, Österreichische Galerie Belvedere, Egon Schiele, *The Family*
Duchamp, Marcel, *Wine Bottle Rack* (1915 original lost)
France, Paris, Musée du Petit Palais, Gustave Courbet, *Self-portrait with a Dog*
Germany, Berlin, Gemäldegalerie, Nicolas Poussin, *Self-portrait*
Germany, Bremen, Paula Modersohn-Becker Museum, Paula Modersohn-Becker, *Self-portrait on my 6th Wedding Anniversary*
Germany, Munich, Alte Pinakothek, Peter Paul Rubens, *Self-portrait with Isabella Brant*
Great Britain, London, Anthony d'Offay Gallery, Andy Warhol, *Self-portrait with Fright Wig*
Great Britain, London, Kenwood House, Rembrandt, *Self-portrait with two Circles*

Great Britain, London, National Gallery, Salvator Rosa, *Self-portrait as Philosophy*

Great Britain, London, National Gallery, Titian, *Allegory of Prudence*

Great Britain, London, National Gallery, Louise Elisabeth Vigée-Lebrun, *Self-portrait in a Straw Hat*

Great Britain, Windsor Castle, Royal Collections, Artemisia Gentileschi, *Self-portrait as the Allegory of Painting*

Italy, Florence, Uffizi Galleries, Rosalba Carriera, *Self-portrait with a Portrait of her Sister*

Netherlands, Amsterdam, Rijksmuseum, Rembrandt, *Self-portrait as the Apostle Paul*

Netherlands, Haarlem, Frans Halsmuseum, Frans Hals, *Banquet of the Officers of the St. George Civic Guard*

Netherlands, Utrecht, Centraal Museum, Mechteld toe Boecop, *Pietà with Self-portrait as Mary-Magdalene*

Spain, Madrid, Centro de Arte Reina Sofia, Salvador Dali, *The Great Masturbator*

USA, Detroit, MI, Institute of Art, Vincent van Gogh, *Self-portrait with Straw Hat*

USA, New York, NY, Frick Collection, Rembrandt, *Self-portrait with Painter's Stick*

USA, New York, NY, Collection of Maria Rodriquez de Reyero, Frida Kahlo, *Self-portrait on the Border of Mexico and the United States*

USA, Washington, D.C., National Gallery of Art, Judith Leyster, *Self-portrait in her Studio*

USA, West Palm Beach, FL, Norton Museum of Art, Paul Gauguin, *Agony in the Garden*

25. **Art and Schools**

BAROQUE   **THE ACADEMY OF FINE ARTS**   **1650-1874**

"I don't know anything about art, but I know what I like." The famous outcry, often heard in the modern art section of the museum, supposes that you have to learn to appreciate art. We agree. But it also supposes that it shouldn't be so, that art should immediately please, even to someone who never takes the trouble to look at it. And only art that pleases immediately would be good. People visit a museum like the shopping mall: I like this, don't like that, that's my favorite color, I hate dogs, I prefer tulips...One may well wonder why art should please in the first place, and to whom.

The idea that you have to learn to understand art is of all times. But how do difficulty and pleasure relate and influence art's evolution? It was no topic in the Middle Ages, when only learned people would control the commissions of the Church or the highest nobility. In the seventeenth century the clientele had become much more varied, along with the different artistic styles. In Holland with its surplus of artists, its booming economy, and well-spread prosperity, it generated the first *art market*. This means that the artist, instead of working on commission, had to produce first, in the hope a customer would show up and pay for a work. The artist had to please, and the competition of the market, where the old masters were sold too, would play the role of judge, which artist was good, which one not, which one expensive, which one not. Also which style should prevail, which subject matter, which size? It explains why there were in Holland painters of landscape, seascape, still-life, flower, genre, house interior, church interior, cityscape, apart from the portrait painters and history painters, all specialists, and why they were so prolific. The middle class became a new client, at some moments outnumbering the old aristocracy and the mercantile patricians (*nouveaux riches*). They showed a preference for small formats and realistic subjects. The intellectually complex history and mythological scenes became rarer. The market decided so.

Now this development was rather particular to the liberal Republic of the Seven United Provinces, usually called Holland. It didn't outlast the seventeenth century. The converging of art and business happened again two centuries later, now all over Europe and North-America. One more century, and it was a global phenomenon. In the meantime another model prevailed, for which the autocratic monarchy of France showed the way.

The greatest political endeavor of the most powerful nation in Europe had been the centralization of all power in the hands of the king. It would not leave the arts alone. On the contrary, they had become a prerogative of the leading class, the aristocracy, who had lost its power, but not its privileges and revenues. Knowledge and enjoyment of the arts became part of its education and its *savoir vivre*. Louis XIV was well versed in all the arts. He and his ministers could only think of them as being strictly in his service, to glorify the kingdom. For the first time we observe here a systematic attempt to integrate the arts in the total program of government. To guarantee the highest quality they were to become part of the school system. Already in 1648 *L'Académie royale de peinture et de sculpture (Royal academy of painting and sculpture)* was founded in Paris, following the early but modest example of the *Accademia di San Luca* in Rome. It was reaching its full mission only after prime-minister Jean-Baptiste Colbert made it in 1662 the premier institution for the glorification of the king.

Its greatest authority and influence were achieved in the sixteen eighties under the directorship of Charles Le Brun. And for the next hundred years the promotion of the arts changed completely. Added to the traditional pedagogy of workshops and apprenticeships, the school proposed lessons, curricula, diplomas, degrees, competitions and prizes. Soon the stamp of the Academy gave students an advantage with potential clients, which weakened the power and influence of the guilds, seen as a threat by the central power. A rational approach of the science of beauty, the publication of its progression and the application of it into teaching, were supposed to prepare the young artists for their task, to serve the advancement of the arts, to refine the general taste and to embellish the capital. Established artists and writers were invited to lecture on the principles of art. The highest award the students competed for was a study trip to Rome, where a beautiful subsidiary academy would welcome them (*Prix de Rome*). Once every two years the students were allowed to show new works with their teachers in the *Salon Carré*, a splendid square hall of the Royal Palace, the Louvre; these were the first art exhibitions. A well-chosen public was invited, art lovers would discuss the talent of some, or the lack thereof of others, and eventually commission well paid portraits or decorations for their mansions. To guide the public, booklets were published with short comments, the earliest show catalogs and art critiques, called *Salon*. Every student was obliged to study some art history, in order to know and retain what the science of art considered best, to reject what it considered worst. A classification and hierarchy of artists and genres was worked out; for instance, Raphael had a better score than Tintoretto, still life as a subject was inferior to a biblical history scene. The general tendency was to recommend above all Antiquity and the Italian Renaissance and with the "moderns" to praise the austere Nicolas Poussin and virile

Annibale Carracci, to recognize the virtuosity of Peter Paul Rubens and to condemn the Dutch contemporary school as a whole. We would say: they encouraged a classical rather than a realistic approach. Art should choose the loftiest subjects described by poetry in solemn style and in so doing elevate itself to the height of the literary art.

The great challenge to try the benefits of this methodology was the new royal palace at Versailles, twenty miles south of Paris. Started in 1668 under the architect Louis Le Vau, continued after 1670 under Jules-Hardouin Mansart, the project had in Europe no equal in size, splendor and costs. Firmly held in hand by the director of the Academy, Charles Le Brun, who was capable of engaging the greatest talents of the country, the colossal enterprise was finished in 1682 as far as architecture and gardens were concerned, while its interior decoration continued for many more years. It was definitely a success in terms of support for the arts and stunning propaganda for Louis XIV and France. Its foremost artistic accomplishments were in architecture, garden design, sculpture, tapestry, furniture and in fact all the decorative arts. It gave France pre-eminence in these fields for two hundred years to come. Painting is not in the list. Did the *Académie* fail in this most individual mode of expression?

The idea of organizing the arts according to the (still rather basic) model of a school of higher learning, with added theoretic instruction, was irresistible in a European continent where the centralizing states developed their grip on the populations and the guilds were seen as potential organizations of popular rebellion. The arts had to serve the new forms of absolutist power. England, Austria, Spain, Russia, and Prussia all founded their Academies that ruled over the arts and architecture, both in instruction and distribution of honors and commissions. From now on art responded to a prescribed ideal of excellence for an aristocratic clientele, later also the higher bourgeoisie. The discipline of the academies governed the arts of Europe from Paris to Saint Petersburg and from London to Vienna and Madrid, not forgetting Munich and Berlin. These fast growing capitals presented vast urban challenges to architects and decorators. The Russian capital of Czar Peter the Great and Czarina Catherine the Great offers us probably the most successful example of city creation from scratch. Washington, D.C. is a more modest but excellent example in the New World. The beauty of many European cities is a lasting tribute to the efficiency of the academies.

In the middle of this happy chorus, one voice is out of tune, however, and we have to come back to the contradiction we stumbled upon earlier, it is essential to our thought. The origin of the academies was the desire to control the art of painting. But it is in painting where they failed and finally had to give up. From the start, in Versailles that is, it became clear that the academic approach was able to make use of painting to decorate, but not to produce *art*. Very soon talented young people tried to escape from the institution's claims; Jean-Antoine Watteau, in the beginning eighteenth century is the first well-known example. Other great artists would follow, like François Boucher and Jean-Baptiste-Siméon Chardin. Membership of the academy soon became more of an honor than a discipline. All the great painters of the eighteenth century, in France and England in particular, used their Academies as the club that confirmed their presence in the social structure. They didn't need the Academy, the Academy needed them. Great decorators, like Giambattista Tiepolo, ignored them completely.

The end of the great era of the academies comes in the nineteenth century. The French Revolution had closed this royal institution (1793), but it made its come back in a stricter form. Jean-Louis David reorganized it to the glory of the Napoleonic Empire and Neo-Classical taste. It survived the fall of the emperor and would keep iron control over the artistic and commercial opportunities of ever growing numbers of adherent painters and sculptors. This control did not stop at questions of administration, but also of painterly style. The Neo-Classical manner, best represented by Jean-Auguste-Dominique Ingres, was as highly advantaged as it was strongly contested by a talented upcoming generation. The number of artists depending on the institution grew steadily, now to be counted in the thousands. The result was that its monopolistic regime came under growing attack in the second half of the century. The principle grievance of the painters was the severe and discriminatory selection of works allowed to be shown in the biannual Salon. The clash came in 1863, when the government of Napoleon III was obliged, by protesting artists and writers, to organize an exhibition for the refused artists, *Le Salon des Refusés*. With this spectacular event modern art was born, and its first leader was Edouard Manet. The first and groundbreaking independent exhibition took place eleven years later, in 1874. It is known as the first Impressionist show, the leader here was Claude Monet.

Paris was undoubtedly the place where it all happened, but similar developments were on their way in the French provinces and in other countries, Britain, Germany, Italy, Austria-Hungary, and the USA. The once-positive stimulating effect of the academies on the arts in Europe was forgotten forever; since then the word *academic* means uninspired. Artists accused academies of ruling against the liberty of self-expression. Not without reason. Schools prefer the obedient student to the rebel talent. They can teach the rules, not genius. Today the academies still exist; not to be washed away, they have radically changed their methods.

In Europe an artist would rarely mention the school where he or she learned his or her craft. Not so in America. The United States, fascinated by the idea of schooling, treats artists like dentists. Because the teaching of art is entrusted to the universities, an artist is often rated by the name of his or her school. One may regret this academic attitude. Notwithstanding, everyone admits that never in any country or age have there been so many students enrolled in the arts programs as in the US today. They receive an *academic* education, often of remarkable quality. It sounds like an idyll and there lies certainly a reason for America's extraordinary contribution to the arts since 1950. However, the American university is a business-controlled institution, and it prepares for careers. Art, alas, can hardly be taught as a career; and the art market is cruel. That is why a vast majority of graduates, immensely talented ones amidst them, part to "find a job," continuing art at best as a hobby. Others find a compromise turning toward applied arts like graphic design, web design, art education or ... the absorbing job of teaching in an art department, preventing most of them from succeeding in an independent career. Here the circle closes on itself.

MAJOR WORKS AND MONUMENTS

Denis Diderot, *Salons* (art criticism)
Immanuel Kant, *Critique of Judgment* (art philosophy)

Roger de Piles, *Balance of Painters* (art connoisseurship)
Joshua Reynolds, *Fifteen Discourses to the Royal Academy* (art theory)

France, Paris, Les Gobelins, tapestry manufactory

France, Paris, Musée du Louvre, Jean-Baptiste-Siméon Chardin, *Basket of Peaches and Glass of Wine*

France, Paris, Musée du Louvre, Jean-Louis David, *The Crowning of Napoleon*

France, Paris, Musée du Louvre, Jean-Auguste-Dominique Ingres, *Turkish Bath (Le Bain Turc)*

France, Paris, Musée du Louvre, Charles Le Brun, *Apollo Gallery* (originally in Versailles)

France, Paris, Musée du Louvre, Pierre Puget, *Milo of Croton*

France, Paris, Musée du Louvre, Hyacinthe Rigaud, *King Louis XIV in coronation costume*

France, Paris, Musée du Louvre, Jean-Antoine Watteau, *Embarkation for Cythère*

France, Paris, Musée d'Orsay, Edouard Manet, *Luncheon on the Grass* (Le déjeuner sur l'herbe)

France, Paris, Sèvres, porcelain manufactory

France, Versailles, Royal Palace, Thomas, François et Pierre-François Francine, *hydraulic works and fountains*

France, Versailles, Royal Palace, André Le Nôtre, (architect), *gardens*

France, Versailles, Royal Palace, André-Charles Boulle, *Chest of drawers for the king's bedroom*

Germany, Berlin, Charlottenburg Museum, Anton Graff, *King Frederic II von Hohenzollern*

Germany, Munich, Alte Pinakothek, François Boucher, *Young Nude Woman on a Bed (Marie-Louise O'Murphy ?)*

Germany, Würzburg, Palace of the Prince-Bishop, Giambattista Tiepolo, *Apollo and the Continents*

Germany, Potsdam, Georg Wenzeslaus von Knobelsdorff (architect), *Royal Palace Sans-Souci*

Great Britain, Hampton Court Royal Palace, Christopher Wren (architect), *South and East wings*

Great Britain, Windsor Castle, Royal Collections, Thomas Gainsborough, *King George III*

Russia, Saint Petersburg, Jean-Baptiste Alexandre Leblond (architect), *Royal Peterhof Palace*

Russia, Saint Petersburg, Senate Square, Etienne Maurice Falconet, *Equestrian statue of Czar Peter the Great*

USA, Washington, D.C., Pierre Charles L'Enfant, *Washington D.C. city plan*

26. **Art and War**

ROMANTIC **GOYA** **1746-1828**

War has always been with us humans. It almost distinguishes our species from others as does art or language. Our judgment of it has varied. Men (that is: males) were traditionally valued as fighters, for women or for food, for their honor, their land, their king or their god. You think, as an educated person of the twenty-first century, that war is the worst of all catastrophes; your opinion is a rather recent one, or it is recent that you can say it and be heard. When you do so, you join the arts, and you honor great artists, Goya to begin with.

Before him, there existed war pictures. The soldier and the artist had served the same kings. Rare were those who understood the Humanist writer Erasmus, who condemned all warfare. The painter Brueghel did. So did Jacques Callot, not sufficiently known, when he started his series of etchings and became the most eloquent and bloodcurdling witness of the Thirty Years' War. They were exceptions to the rule. Art echoed the victor's law, or the ruler's rhetoric. War, the ruler would claim, was an art, a science, an excitement, a career, a prize, and glory. Art illustrated this in faithful imitation, obedience or even enthusiasm. If we put apart as crafts all kinds of beautifully wrought weapons, in wood and metal since the dawn of humanity, paintings of battles on the land or the sea were a common genre since the Renaissance and considered handsome decorations on the walls of a palace. Notice that there are few masterpieces. You might know, by the Florentine Paolo Uccello, the courageous *Battle of San Romano,* now torn into three pieces between three museums; or the inimitable *Battle of Alexander at Issus,* a masterpiece by Dürer's colleague

Albrecht Altdorfer. This same battle was already a famous subject in antiquity, as a Roman mosaic proves. Maybe you've seen the stunning pen paintings by Willem van de Velde of the sea battles fought (and won) by Dutch seamen against the Brits; later this painter moved to London and did the same for the British victories, earning more money and fame on the other side of the North Sea. We see fighting in art, a fascinating subject in sculpture, like the *Battle of Gods and Titans,* on the Altar of Pergamum, now in Berlin; and the *Battle of the Centaurs*, by young Michelangelo. And also the *Battle of the Ten Nudes,* a curious engraving by Pollaiuolo. That is not war, it is metaphor. And there is allegory: you've heard of Rubens' literary mythological treatment of the theme, of course, *The Disasters of War,* opposing Venus and Mars, Love and War, and in their wake wealth or desolation, the arts or destruction.

War, real war, changed from glory to disaster in the few years between the French Revolution, 1789, and the fall of Napoleon, 1815. In the middle of that turbulent period, Francisco de Goya was a painter at the Spanish court, the most archaic of Europe and also the most corrupt. The king proved utterly unable to stop the French when the Emperor sent an army to occupy the country. Then the people started a long guerilla war.

Until the beginning of the nineties, Francisco de Goya had been a quite typical but prolific happy-go-Rococo artist, hard-working and so earning palace and church decorations or portraits of the noblemen. A slow but faultless career had brought him from a mediocre provincial position to the court where he climbed the social ladder to becoming the first painter to the king. This ultimate success coincides with definite changes in the man and his art. First of all he became deaf and as somber spirited as Ludwig van Beethoven in the same years in another art in another major capital in Europe, Vienna. And as with this musical colleague, every one of his works now was a step away from established forms and all in the direction of modern art. Goya assumed a double career, one might say, a public one and a personal one; and he was able to be authentic in both. The personal one studied the mind from the outside, in intimate oils depicting insane asylums, prisons, hospitals, tribunals, and in etchings depicting border line human behavior (*Los Caprichos,* 1798). The public one studied politics from the inside. Goya, as portraitist at the court, was admitted in the inner circle of influential men and women. In 1800 the king Charles IV (or rather the queen Luisa) placed a commission for a *Royal Family* portrait in the tradition of *Las Meninas.* Never a painter before him had succeeded in marrying in one work the splendor of the past to the spiritual decadence of the present: a frightening master work of ambiguity. There was the over-ambitious prime minister and the queens favorite, Manuel de Godoy, who ordered from the painter a daring nude (plus an equally daring dressed version of the same model) and a portrait, subtitled *The Prince of Peace;* it was not the painter's fault that within a few years this subtitle turned into pure irony. The fall of Spain was partly due to this man. Godoy's condemnation for treason brought Goya however before the tribunal of the Inquisition! The following French invasion was rapid and terrifying. During the four years of occupation of the country, the painter stayed in Madrid. There he encountered the reality of war. For once a man looked it right in the face. He couldn't turn his eye away from it. And art declared war on war. The first strike was brilliant. Not in painting but in etching and aquatint, a humble technique, executed in secret, no royal consent but personal investment, Goya performed a series of eighty-two compositions depicting the *Disasters of War.* It took him five years. These compositions are as eye-opening as if no one had ever seen war before. Here are no battles, no strategies or rhetoric of marshals, no generals on horseback, no band or flag or standard, no soldiers in order of attack, no laughing girls or camp fires, no comfortable tents of the officers, no puffs of gunpowder above the trees along the creek in the valley, no heroism. With a few strokes of his etching needle, Goya sends those to the reserves of the art museum as illustrations for history books. No victorious armies, no singing crowds. No politics, no ideology, no ideal, no sense. Only the cruelty of man to man, to soldier, to peasant, Spaniard, Frenchman, woman, child, animal, nature, in a rage of destruction. Even 200 years after, each image is grim, each image suffocates us, making us whisper that such is man making war, and war making man. There is no escape, no happy conclusion. Each man is both victim and tormentor, martyr and torturer, violating and violated, each one devil and desperate, crazy and dangerous, vile and villainous, barbarous and beast. It is a realistic picture. There is no humanity left on the ruins of war.

The style of the etchings is rude, chaotic, primitive, like the subject they present. And prophetic. It tolls for the end of *illusion* in art as well as in politics. It marks the beginning of the end of a man-centered epoch, which Leonardo had coined in his famous drawing, the *Vitruvian Man*. Man had lost control that was so well symbolized by *perspective*. Perspective and illusion cannot be the pillars of art anymore. And beauty could not be its goal anymore, nor its guide. The war had broken them. The *Disasters* confronted art with reality. Art was not anymore a view in another world, but in ours. Art here shows not the invisible, but the unseen; reveals not the unthinkable, but the unthought-of.

A new epoch starts and one thing is clear: art can't assume its old role in the service of a warlord. Art from now is against war. The artist accepts to be the conscience of his age. We call that age modern.

Francisco de Goya is the Pilgrim Father of modern art. On his symbolic *Mayflower* he leaves behind the old world of the illusions of European man, which had grown into self-sufficiency, colonialism, imperialism and permanent warfare. Goya works it out in a cruelly visionary painting in 1812; it is called *The Third of May*. Its subject is an event of Mai 3, 1808. Here is no place left for allegory or mythology, although it is as symbolic as Jerome Bosch's *Last Judgment* or Matthias Grünewald's *Crucifixion*. It shows the cold-blooded execution by a firing squad of what the French army must have called Spanish terrorists. It has not lost a drop since of its terror nor actuality.

Goya did not cry out in the desert, though it might have seemed so. His etchings were not published and his paintings were not visible. The new Spanish government was even more reactionary than before the French war. It ultimately made Goya search exile in France, Bordeaux, where he died. Before that, he lived in a small home in the suburbs of Madrid: *La Quinta del Sordo*, it was called, the House of the Deaf Man. Mostly shunning from politics, he pursued his lonely adventure into an art without the support of tradition.

His paintings, often directly done on the walls of the house, like murals in a prehistoric grotto, are the darkest works, literally and figuratively, of the entire European artistic heritage. Haunted images, forms unintelligible but speaking to all, alienated and strange but familiar to our nightmares, they are a poignant illustration of his own dictum, a warning for our times: *The Sleep of Reason Awakens Demons* (etching).

But he had not cried out in the desert. His works were signs of the times and not isolated. The first French artists had joined the peace corps. Already in 1808, Baron Antoine-Jean Gros was severely criticized for showing more compassion with the suffering of Prussian soldiers than admiration for Napoleon's victory in his rendering of the *Battle of Eylau*. In 1818 Théodore Géricault delivered his masterpiece, *The Raft of the Medusa*, as a powerful indictment against criminal corruption of the government. A few years later Eugène Delacroix protested in the middle of the Salon against the cruelties in the war between Greeks and Turks. In May 1831, a year after a popular uprising in Paris, he hung in the Salon his famous *Liberty Leading the People*, the source model for the *Statue of Liberty*. In it is a self-portrait: the artist carries a gun. From here on art is on the barricades for peace.

MAJOR WORKS AND MONUMENTS

Adams, Eddie, *Vietnamese General Executing Vietcong* (photography)

Callot, Jacques, *Miseries of War* (etchings)

France, Paris, Musée du Louvre, Antoine-Jean Baron Gros, *Napoleon on the Battlefield of Eylau*

France, Paris, Musée du Louvre, Eugène Delacroix, *Scenes from the Massacre at Scio*

France, Paris, Musée du Louvre, Eugène Delacroix, *Liberty Leading the People*

France, Paris, Musée du Louvre, Théodore Géricault, *The Raft of the Medusa*

France, Paris, Musée Picasso, Pablo Picasso, *Massacres in Korea*

Germany, Mannheim, Kunsthalle, Edouard Manet, *Execution of Emperor Maximilian*

Goya, Francisco de, *Los Caprichos* (etchings)

Goya, Francisco de, *Disasters of War* (etchings)

Italy, Florence, Casa Buonarroti, Michelangelo, *Battle of the Centaurs*

Italy, Florence, Uffizi Galleries, Peter Paul Rubens, *Venus and Mars or the Horrors of War*

Netherlands, Amsterdam, Rijksmuseum, Willem van de Velde, *The Battle of Ter Heyde*

Spain, Madrid, Prado Museum, Pieter Brueghel the Elder, *Triumph of Death*

Spain, Madrid, Prado Museum, Francisco de Goya, *Third of May 1808*

Spain, Madrid, Prado Museum, Francisco de Goya, *La Maja Vestida*

Spain, Madrid, Prado Museum, Francisco de Goya, *Saturn Devouring his Child*
Spain, Madrid, Prado Museum, Francisco de Goya, *Family portrait of Charles IV, King of Spain*
USA, New York, NY, Frédéric-Auguste Bartholdi, *Statue of Liberty*

USA, Chicago, Art Institute, Marc Chagall, *White Crucifixion*
USA, Collection of Fred Koeler, Frederic Edwin Church, *Our Banner in the Sky*

27. **Art and the Nation**

THE ART MUSEUM   **1750 - today**

We were all born in a nation; we were given a nationality like a birthmark, which will follow us all our life. We think it is natural and are surprised to learn that the idea of the nation as your country is a quite novel invention. Joan of Arc never fought for France, even less for its nation, but for the House of France, its dynasty, against the House of England. The American Declaration of Independence (1776) and the French Revolution (1789) were the events that promoted the birth of the national idea most successfully.

Similarly, when we think of art, we think of a museum. Again, this seems so overwhelmingly evident, that we are surprised to learn that the museum is a quite recent institution. The rise of nations and that of art museums are closely linked.

Originally art belonged to a place. The place could be a mountain or a cavern, or a temple on the mountain, a town in the plains, a palace in the town or a statue in the temple. People, from the king to the slave, would have the care of it. Don't think the pyramids belonged to a Pharaoh, not more or less than the Nile did. Not more or less than the Temple of Solomon belonged to Solomon, or *Banqueting House* to Charles I, king of England and Scotland, who ordered its interior decoration. They belonged to the place, with the soil and the water and the air and the stars; call it Egypt or Israel or Great-Britain. They belonged to it just like the people and the kings and the gods; even more so than the people, because they would never move (or die). They *were* that place, that country, physically; and symbolically too, they were its soul. That's why it's art. Golden bracelets, silver earrings, plates or knives of daily use, however beautiful, would never be (or have) a soul (not art but craft, in our terms). They could move like people, from people to people. On the contrary, the seven-branch Menorah of pure gold would never be moved; this candle-stand belonged to the Temple, which belonged to the mountain Sion, to Jerusalem, to Israel. It *was* Israel, both country and people, its soul made visible (typically art). Imagine the trauma of 586 BCE! The Babylonians destroyed the country, the city, the Temple, and deported the entire population to Babylon. They *moved* the Menorah; they moved it away from Jerusalem. Did it become, on the road to the Euphrates, nothing but well-crafted gold again? Did it lose its soul? The Babylonians would say yes. The Jews would say no. And a century later, in rebuilt Jerusalem, in the new Temple there was a new Menorah. Some maintained it was the old one; the soul of the people and its country could not be destroyed, not even by Babylonians.

More than two thousand years later, in London on the Thames, King Charles I was beheaded on behalf of Oliver Cromwell, 1649. His family was dismissed and his fortune requested by the new state. Britain was suddenly a republic. However, although it was a pure celebration of Charles's father James, who unified Scotland and England, the beautiful ceiling of Banqueting House, painted by Rubens, was left untouched. That art work *was* already the country, it wouldn't move, until today. Had nothing changed since the pyramids? Some things had. The question rose, indeed, what to do with Charles's *private art* collection, to whom belonged, for example the self-portrait he obtained from Rubens personally, when he was only Prince of Wales. Or his portraits as the King of Britain on horseback by Van Dyck. Two hundred years earlier such a problem wouldn't have existed. Kings had no *art*. They only had gold and silver and precious stones, so to say, necklaces and rings, plates and knives. Apart from their throne, crown and scepter, which they had on loan, from the country, for life. In terms of art they would order an altar piece, a huge one for the cathedral, a small one for personal worship in their personal chapel. It would belong to the chapel and never leave it (ideally). In which chapel there were already numberless older religious artworks, and relics and other bric-a-brac, giving sense and prestige to the place, never to leave.

But in the course of the fifteenth century, art works of a new type, instead of staying attached to their soil, encroached upon the category of commodities, of moveable and saleable goods. Tempera and oil, small panels and especially canvases, easy to carry, were at the origin of this change, combined with changing demand in subject matter, portraits especially. Portraits move with the sitters and their families. Paintings and sculptures had become more similar to necklaces and rings, plates and knives. Indeed, since the sixteenth century we see private people collect paintings, sculptures, drawings and other art. No people collected with more passion than the rulers of Europe, emperors and kings, aristocrats and other governors and ministers. During three centuries the Hapsburg and the Bourbon families, the Hohenzollern and the Wittelsbach, the Tudor and the Stuart, the Savoy and the Orange and a dozen other families amassed dazzling collections of art works (as well as of other curiosities), privately owned. Just like they collected, by marriages and wars, regions with their populations, which they privately owned and over which they privately ruled. It was a top heavy world. Louis XIV put it in an cynical aphorism, he probably believed in as his credo: "The State is I." He could be equally ruthless in expecting art works, owned by his subjects, to join the reserves of his personal, though royal, collections.

The enlightened 18th century, philosophers and rulers alike, realized that essential changes were taking place in the relation between art, its public and its owners. Some of the philosophers, like Denis Diderot or Immanuel Kant, wrote extensively on art, creating the philosophical discipline of aesthetics, which tempts to present art as if there were no ownership at all. Some of the princes opened one of their many houses or even had a special gallery built in order to allow the public to admire part of their art possessions, one afternoon per week.

The French Revolution (1789), toppling the old social system in many ways, drew also the most radical conclusions in our domain, the arts. The king had to render his land, his people, his palaces and his art collection. From now on the land of France belonged to the *nation* and the nation belonged to the French people. Even, the people *were* the nation. Part of this land were its monuments and its art; they were handed over to the nation. The Louvre was converted from the royal palace into the *national* museum. Here the artistic treasures of all the national territory would be gathered, conserved and exhibited for the enjoyment and instruction of all. Its rule was to be open to the public, every day. One day in the week (the still traditional Tuesday) it was open only to artists; they would copy the masters of old in order to learn from the best. The art of the nation would guide the young artists as well as the people toward a better national future.

Tragically, as in the case of so many good ideas of the French Revolution, this noble birth of the museum coincided with the massive destruction of the places that formerly belonged to art and where the art belonged: countless monasteries, churches, castles and mansions of the nobility. Above all medieval art suffered from the barbarity of ignorance and hate. The most painful memory of this wave of destruction is kept by the minimal rests of the Romanesque monastery of Cluny, once the greatest of all Christianity. While buildings were sold or destroyed, the "best" portable pieces would be moved to Paris, ripped off from their birth place, like orphans.

The French nation sacked its own country. A stream of treasures filled the vaults of the new art temple, the Louvre Museum, which opened in 1793. It was the national treasure; like the crown jewels had been in a dynasty. More than that: it was the nation made visible. Art played its role, it made the invisible visible. Now it represented the nation and enhanced the notion of national unity inside the new borders.

Only a few years later, Napoleon, who had not only the dream of a united Europe under his leadership, had a grandiose vision for art too: assemble all the continent's master pieces in one place, the Paris museum. Again art had to serve (and suffer) the new political world view. The stream of French art works that were already on the roads became a wide European river flowing over the whole continent to the Louvre in the heart of Paris. In the middle of the wars waged by the Empire, carts full of the most precious paintings and sculptures, slowly drawn by oxen and asses, left Rome and Florence and crossed the snow covered Alps; left Munich and Hanover and crossed the roaring Rhine; or left Ghent and Bruges and plowed through the rainy fields of Flanders, in the direction of the Seine. The overflow was sent forth to the Museums of Fine Arts in the provinces, founded since 1801 in the major cities of the country, including temporarily Brussels and Antwerp. For one decade the greatest European art show drew artists and art lovers from all corners of fighting Europe over to the Louvre, even from Britain. It was the first time that in one place the works from totally different countries could be seen together, and the styles of different schools and periods could be compared. Here we can situate the germ of the discipline of art history.

When Napoleon was defeated, the victorious powers showed little appreciation for his idea of the Louvre. They saw of course nothing but the brutal looting of their age old treasures; they commanded them back. And the river of art flew stream upwards:

the *Mystic Lamb* to Ghent, the Dürer portraits to Munich, the Raphael *Cartoons* (drawings for tapestries) to the Vatican, the *Birth of Venus* to Florence, etc., etc...

Nevertheless, the idea of the *nation*, exalted by the national *art* museum, was too powerful to be abandoned. In the nineteenth century we see in the capital of every (often brand new) nation in Europe the foundation of a national collection of art works and in the heart of the city the erection of a monumental "temple" to house it, designed by a major national architect. The core of the collection came from the possessions of the reigning family, often still on the throne. Now the works became inalienable, they were again immobilized. This is how many a famous art museum in Europe came into being. Include here Munich, Dresden, Berlin, Vienna, Florence, Milan, Naples, Budapest, Prague, St. Petersburg, Lisbon, Madrid, Copenhagen, Stockholm, The Hague and many more. Amsterdam and London followed a little later, but the British Museum preceded the Louvre by 40 years. (Rome had been the first with the Capitoline Museums of antique art, open since 1734!).

Not really an art museum, the British Museum received its most famous pieces, the Parthenon marbles just after the end of the Napoleonic wars. Lord Elgin, the British ambassador to the Ottoman Empire, certainly convinced that he was saving them from local neglect and Ottoman disdain, paid for "excavating" them, made drawings and casts and shipped them between 1800 and 1812, maneuvering between pirates, storms, shipwreck and the French fleet, from Athens to London. There he was seriously accused of vandalism by some. But the national feeling was seriously flattered and that prevailed. Didn't the French do the same? And the Prussians? The Italians? Everybody indeed! Europe seemed to have decided to empty the Middle East of its artistic heritage. The Westminster Parliament voted to pay half (!) of the asked price for Phidias' masterpieces and offered them to the British Museum, where they have been on show without interruption until today. Regularly, but in vain, the Greek government asks for the return to the home country of its emblematic national heritage.

As these examples show, the nature and spirit of museums were set from the beginning; in spite of all appearances in their growing complexity they have not changed since. Art raises national pride, identity and consciousness. The collections are of two sorts: the national school and the pieces of *universal* art, *i.e.* art historically recognized as such. Together they enhance the national prestige. And nations pay for it. Here the art works are in good hands, by the way; they are taken excellent care of by trained experts, who have overcome by their very trade prejudice and ignorance. The physical conditions are adapted to the art's needs and all the sciences are called for assistance to protect their well-being and longevity. The museum pays a huge contribution to the memory of all mankind in a world that otherwise often rushes to destruction. The respect of the various origins of admired art works enhances like no other factor the respect for the people who are the descendants of their makers and cherish their culture.

As soon as museums opened, art was organized in schools and epochs, in styles and techniques, expressing history and geography, comparing nations with nations, peoples with peoples, governments with governments, the past with the present moment.

In a place where it was cut off from its origin, art's own value criteria changed. For a large but tenacious public, art is reduced to its beauty alone (according to certain obviously subjective norms, constantly put to the test by new artists and art historians). For a marginal minority art is only for art's sake. Fluctuating market value is always food for the sensational press, but the museum must keep a keen eye on it.

In the museum an art work starts a life which is defined by the museum and its politics, more than by the artist. Its new, usually unpronounced role, generated by the museum, was and is before all to signify the nation's existence, to glorify the nation's past and presence, and to educate the visitors, teaching them the nation's values. The historical or actual significance and authenticity of the work has become the matter for experts. Oscillating constantly between defenders of art for art's sake and those of educational purposes, the museum can only be inscribed in the political agenda of all possible national regimes. Even in the twentieth century, when modern art was made to be ultimately (or immediately!) shown in nation owned museums, nationalism was the undercurrent of museum building, aiming at the national *subconscious* of artists and visitors. The brutally *conscious* exceptions were tyrannical regimes, such as Nazi Germany, the Soviet Union or Fascist Italy. Their art is seen as a failure in artistic terms.

The ideological mixture of art for art's sake and patriotic political investment proved to be of great efficiency worldwide in the twentieth century. America, where in the last hundred years great capital amassed by business was and is invested in splendid art collections, adopted the model whole heartedly. It introduced the possibility for wealthy citizens, not only to drastically write off their taxes, but also to have their names immortalized by the founding and sponsoring of art museums or the "naming" of galleries in the museum. Washington, D.C. received the National Gallery of Art in 1937; its main collections were donated by large private holdings, notably Paul Mellon's. Many believe that the Metropolitan Museum in New York is the national museum, the only one that can compete with the biggest institutions in Europe, like the Hermitage, the Prado or the Louvre; but it came into being privately, founded by citizens in 1870; this status hasn't changed. The last spectacular foundations in museum land America are the J. Paul Getty Museum in Malibu, CA, and the Museum of American Art in Crystal Bridges, AR. The last one was funded by an heir of the Walmart fortunes, and founded in the middle of nowhere, as one might think: it will change the whole Mid-West! In Europe the number of museums equally multiplied by the hundreds. The most interesting historical phenomenon however is the adherence to this nation-building precept in the new independent states in Africa and Asia. The smallest and poorest decolonized country has its art museum, as has the richest, of course. To name a spectacular example in this last category, it would be the new Louvre Museum in Abu Dhabi, one of the United Emirates; it seems fascinating that an Islamic state, where the religion in principle prohibits images, needs an art museum to really exist.

P.S. I almost forgot to tell that the collection of pictures acquired by King Charles I was dispersed. Rubens' *Self-portrait* stayed however in the royal collections. One of Van Dyck's equestrian portraits toured Europe before returning to Britain in 1706 and to the National Gallery in 1885. Another one landed in France and is now in the Louvre.

MAJOR WORKS AND MONUMENTS

Austria, Vienna, Kunsthistorisches Museum, Titian, *The Antiquarian Jacopo Strada*

France, Paris, Musée du Louvre, Michelangelo, *Rebellious Slave* and *Dying Slave*

France, Paris, Musée du Louvre (since 1808), Agasias of Ephesos, *Nude Warrior* (so called *Borghese Gladiator*)

France, Paris, Musée du Louvre, Anthony van Dyck, *Charles I, King of Great Britain*

France, Paris, Musée du Louvre (since 1808), Paolo Veronese, *Wedding at Cana*

Great Britain, London, Banqueting House of Whitehall Palace, Peter Paul Rubens, Ceiling painting of the *Celebration of the Reign of King James I*

Great Britain, London, National Gallery, Anthony van Dyck, *Charles I on Horseback*

Great Britain, London, National Gallery, unknown French artist, *"Wilton Diptych"*, Altarpiece of King Richard II

Great Britain, London, Royal Collections, Peter Paul Rubens, *Self-portrait with Hat*

USA, Malibu, CA, J. Paul Getty Museum, Vincent van Gogh, *The Irises*

28. **Art as the Eye**
   (Impression)

IMPRESSIONISM   MONET-PISSARRO-RENOIR-SISLEY   1850-1915

Seen (and heard) on TV: "The eye is the organ that defines best the human race." It sounded so evident; nobody protested. In fact, it seems evident only since two or three centuries in Europe. That is not quite the human race. Some seven or eight generations ago our relation with the visual world changed. Before that, grown up in the Christian faith, we didn't trust our eyes, we trusted the Bible. We were disciples of the apostle Paul (and the philosopher Plato). Sight is a sense, and the senses were inferior to reason. Good advice: check well before you believe your eyes.

In the nineteenth century that had changed. The advice was now: Check *with your eyes* before you believe. Check the Bible to start with. And you will *see*.

Sciences were based on seeing. Certainly, the arts had shown the way. Take a patient look at a *Garland of Flowers and Fruit for a Portrait of William III of Orange* by Jan Davidszoon de Heem, in Lyons Museum, and count, if you can, the different plants, many dozens of them; some are well-known, some exotic, some from far away countries, some from the backyard; see how well they are observed, described in every part, from young exemplars in the bud, to others at the top of their strength and beauty, to old ones, losing their petals, dying, a life in three steps; add the fruits and some butterflies and caterpillars, some flies and snails you get them for the same price. These artists showed powerfully the way to a Carl Linnaeus, when he analyzed all nature and classified it in a scientific manner, *i.e.* based on observation alone. Now only the eye could overthrow a thesis taken for granted. For instance that witches flew on broomsticks through the night and played dirty games with the devil. The eye was the great verifier, the arbiter. Fewer women were burnt at the stake (for witch craft at least). Although today the sciences have left the eye far behind, they are still based on seeing, we still trust in them, and that trust dates from the nineteenth century.

Is it by chance that photography was invented in the same time? You *believe* a photo; you can't help it, even if you know it is manipulated. You *inspect* a drawing, and probably *suspect* it. In fact, you always suspected art! Well, you were probably right.

How strange that photography soon after its invention was rejected from the list of the fine arts for 150 years. Were photos *too* true? Possibly. Or *too* real? What is the difference? The intervention of an apparatus, of machinery, of technology, condemned photography to reality. Apparently people expressed the feeling that the human hand alone could make art. And that art was not reality. People started to see the *hand* in analog photography with its "silver gelatin" prints, only since the invention of the digital technology. Now the history of photography is an integral part of the history of art.

Is it by chance that just after the invention of photography the term realist was (finally) used in art critical texts, and that the first high profile art movement that emerged then was called Realism? Gustave Courbet was its valiant defender in word (*The Realist Manifesto,* 1855) and work (*The Painter's Studio: A Real Allegory*). Realism was the veritable stepping stone for the Impressionist revolution.

Claude Monet, Pierre-Auguste Renoir, Paul Cézanne, Alfred Sisley, all the great Impressionists, were born in the very years Louis

Daguerre launched the first camera on the market, 1839–1840. (Only Camille Pissarro was ten years older.) This typical product of science and technology, following the invention of a mechanically produced image by Nicéphore Niepce in 1826, re-invented in the following years by William Henry Fox Talbot in England, is in fact a big simplified eye. A lens captures the rays of light reflected by an object and carries them to a sensitive emulsion; it forms an image by *interpreting* the rays (chemical reaction) according to their degree of luminosity. Thirty years later the Parisian artists mentioned above behaved like living cameras. They developed a style that would record in paint the reflection of light on the world as seen by the eye and offered to the brain for an interpretation.

This was a revolutionary approach of the art of painting. Inspired by scientific method.

Painting, they would say, is about seeing, so let it be nothing else. Let it be the hand of the eye. Let it be objective. Let it be the practice of study and analysis of light, without which we wouldn't see at all; so let us work in the sun, outside that is (*plein air,* in French), even if it rains. Any subject is fine to be painted, because it is not the subject we paint, but the light that creates it in our eye. So let us paint subjects around us, today, because we don't know how things looked a century ago, let alone twenty. Landscapes or river or sea or cityscapes are our favorites, rather than nudes in an attic or studio (however *piquant*, my dear). Let us study the colors, because the light speaks to us in the language of colors. See how different red is next to yellow from red next to green (it's a rose, my darling, accidentally). Let us study how colors interact. How they complement each other, that means strengthen or weaken each other. Colors do nothing else (just like people, you know...). We study it with our eyes, on the spot. Like scientists report their observations in the lab, so do we in a painting: with our brushes, on the canvas, ready on the stretcher, and the paint, ready in the tubes. We have to recreate those hues by juxtaposing colors on the linen, shorts strokes and long ones, you can see them if you approach, take a look, we've nothing to hide, one next to the other, not always mixing them on the palette, not even on the canvas. That is what our teachers hate! But if you look from a distance, they merge in your eye (not the teachers, silly, but the hues). And see now how fresh it looks, the tone is very high, but isn't it like that in nature? And isn't the day more interesting than the night (sorry, my dear) and noon more happy than dusk? For the eye! Away with moody dark paintings! We prefer sunrise to sunset. See how the shadows play with the colors and how there is no such a thing as grey, if you pay attention (please, pay attention); so why would we ever put grey paint on our palette? Difficult, but refreshing. And speaking about form, our eyes can't tell the outline of a thing or person. In fact, there are no outlines, as the teachers at the academy want us so badly to believe, there are only colors that meet. We will not draw lines, then, but promptly sketch with the brush. And then, when you are on the river, or in the fields or on the hills, or in the city, there is not much perspective either, not in the eye at least (in the brain, yes, *mon amie*), there is just a horizon, and for the rest there are colors that meet. It makes the world as flat as a palette board. Even a lovely person (oh, my dearest) is nothing but flat color stains (and therefore so lovely). The person moves, the colors of her dress change in the grass; the sun moves too, and the colors change more. Let us concentrate now, not talk, not even think, we have to paint, to paint fast and like a snapshot capture the light of a second, so the picture will forever vibrate in the eye (your beloved eye). Because today will never come back (though you may, dear).

What you read in a minute, Monet and Co. needed 10, 20, or 30 years to discover and to transpose it into painting. The resistance was great. They had to battle against academic colleagues, journalists and the public opinion; their constant fight against malice or indifference, sarcasm or skeptics was heroic for our time and set a paradigm for modern art. Financial hardship was their lot, becoming proverbial in the field, sometimes of the legendary kind, though in some cases, yes: Alfred Sisley, the purest maybe of all Impressionists, had to die at sixty before his paintings began to sell at all. But these painters were the first moderns; they broke new terrain when they tried to limit the act of painting to the pure act of seeing, without allowing the mood or psyche or brain or traditions to influence them. In doing so they tried to liberate art from all metaphysics or imagination or subjectivity, and from all academic tricks and recipes, believing in the validity of nature seen by an objective eye. They tried to make art a progressive force, worthy of its time, part of its age, pointing to the future, confident in human resources and dedicated to a wide public. They did all that.

The performance of the Impressionists has been to start the art of painting naively from scratch, to take nature as a guide and light as the source of inspiration. Their mix of candid simplicity and potential depth was based on the love of nature and faith in human endeavors. The world has received from their hands its first global style.

Very soon we see the neighboring countries of France, strengthened by the Parisian boldness, develop their own anti-academic movements, similar to Impressionism but responding to local conditions. The Netherlands were very successful, even internationally, with what we call The Hague School; the Maris' brothers and Joseph and Isaac Israëls, father and son, reestablished the reputation of the Dutch school. In Italy a similar rebirth was achieved by a group called the *Macchiaioli.* In England we see the *Pre-Raphaelites,* different in their goals, start the battle with conventional art. Two countries stand out as having developed a continuing Impressionist painting culture, almost a cult: Russia and the USA. They have built the best collections of masterpieces by the founders of the style. In all those countries, without forgetting the middle European and Scandinavian ones, these movements were like the necessary upbeat for more determining revolutions to come in the beginning of the next century

There is irony hidden in the formidable effort and success of the Impressionists.

The intense and unique concentration of the Impressionists on nature and its forms or apparitions may have brought them far from traditional European metaphysics and academic standards, but close to oriental forms of spirituality. Pantheism and Zen-Buddhism were growing fashions of thought in the nineteenth century. Manet, Degas, Monet, and other leading artists were fascinated by Japanese culture and collected avidly Japanese prints and artefacts. Monet even conceived a mesmerizing Japanese water garden behind his house in Giverny. In other words, the atheist Claude Monet was a very spiritual artist. His art was pure contemplation, an old idea in Europe. It showed (it saw) what no eye had ever seen, revealing the truth about nature sounding its hidden secrets. His words are rational, but his paintings are almost visionary: grain stacks like rainbows, water lilies like lightning in the mirror of a pond, trains in the city like apparitions in the night. And we have seen that the quasi mystical fascination with light is not new either, it is constancy in Europe, through Byzantine, Gothic and Baroque art. Wherever our starting point, when we follow the circle of life, we arrive at the same illuminations, because we

are stepped in our profound humanity, our beautiful limitations.
However old the world. art makes us new.

MAJOR WORKS AND MONUMENTS

France, Paris, Musée Marmottan Monet, Claude Monet, *Impression Sunrise* (Impression, soleil levant)

France, Paris, Musée de l'Orangerie, Claude Monet, *Les Nymphéas* (The Water Lilies)

France, Paris, Musée d'Orsay, Gustave Courbet, *The Painter's Studio : A Real Allegory of a Seven Year Phase in my Artistic and Moral Life*

France, Paris, Musée d'Orsay, Camille Pissarro, *The Red Roofs*

France, Paris, Musée d'Orsay, Pierre-Auguste Renoir, *Moulin de la Galette*

France, Pau, Musée des Beaux-Arts, Edgar Degas, *A Cotton Office in New Orleans*

France, Rouen, Musée des Beaux-Arts, Claude Monet, *Rouen Cathedral*

Germany, Frankfurt, Museum Städel, Max Liebermann, *Free Hour in the Amsterdam Orphanage*

Great Britain, London, Courtauld Institute of Art, Camille Pissarro, *Lordship Lane Station, Dulwich*

Hungary, Budapest, Hungarian National Gallery, Karoly Ferenczy, *Boys Throwing Pebbles into the River*

Netherlands, The Hague, Museum Mesdag, Isaac Israëls, *Donkey Ride on the Beach*

Netherlands, The Hague, Panorama Museum, Hendrik Willem Mesdag, *Panorama of Scheveningen*

Russia, Moscow, State Tretyakow Gallery, Vasily Polenov, *Moscow Courtyard*

Russia, Moscow, State Tretyakow Gallery, Ilya Repin, *Mikhail Glinka Composing the Opera "Ruslan and Lyudmila"*

Russia, St. Petersburg, Hermitage Museum, Alfred Sisley, *Village on the Banks of the Seine*

29. **Art as the Soul**

(Expression)

POST-IMPRESSIONISM & SYMBOLISM RODIN-VAN GOGH 1875–1925

Is the essence of art input or output? That is the underlying topic of this lesson.

In the Renaissance view that dominated Western culture from 1400 until 1900, art is a mirror. It reflects faithfully the *input* it receives from reality and narratives. Many art schools had embraced that point of view. Impressionism tried to give it a modern formula: *the eye* is the mirror, and art is nothing but an eye (*cf.* Cézanne à propos de Monet).

For the vast majority of museum visitors Impressionism means something else: it is the imprecise *blurred* manner, it gives *only a vague impression* of things, hence the name (wrong!). An unsmooth mirror, so to say, an unfocused camera. Curiously, that kind of painting exists, best implemented by the Romantic English sea-storm-and-twilight painter Joseph M. W. Turner. He produced imaginary, literary, lyrical and heavily emotional works in a fog-like manner. His use of color and light was inspired by symbolic statements found in Goethe; it is speculative, subjective, with dreamlike, almost abstract results. And since we quote the name of the German poet, a contemporary German painter, Caspar David Friedrich, was second to none in giving to landscape painting new philosophic breadth, idealistic and transcendental. The Impressionists (and John Constable in England before them) tried to go beyond this and deal with the landscape in a real, painterly, and objective way; modern, in one word. They analyzed light in the scientific tradition of Isaac Newton and the recent studies of M. C. Chevreuil. But today the public puts them all in the same *blurred* basket. And it continues to *admire* Jean-Auguste-Dominique Ingres, the painstaking academic painter of nudes: *"That's what the world really looks like!"*

How to make sense of this? We have to go back to the mirror and the eye.

Our eye sees, but our brain filters. We "see", therefore, what we *think* or *expect* or *choose* to see. We live with prejudice. The image of the world is formed before we see it. That is what Ingres painted and the public admires: a recognizable and recognized selection of reality. As soon as we begin to see without prejudice, the resulting image is *blurred*. The eye is as yet unfocused, like the new-born's eye. Reality is too rich. In fact, the image in art became blurred because art was no mirror of the world anymore. Impressionism was a last attempt. Its subject was not *what* we see but *how* we see it. It was also a first attempt: as the human society had radically changed, Impressionism had started to update art to modern man. The next generation set indeed the next step in the discovery of this modern being. Not by studying the outside anymore but the inside. Art turned the mirror towards the soul or the psyche. It became curious again of the mind. Not objective in-formation counted first, but subjective trans-formation.

In art history this revolution is brought about by two movements, one called Post-Impressionism, the other Symbolism. They cross fertilize each other.

First there was a moment of transition, an attempt to bring the Impressionist mission to a good end in its own terms. There seemed to be good reason to explore further the rational approach of painting as the study of light. The name given to the new style was Neo-Impressionism; the young Georges Seurat was its inventor and fearless leader, while the older Camille Pissarro became a strong supporter for a time. This time the outcome left no doubt about the intentions: objective color analysis was combined with a rigorously impersonal brush stroke. No strokes, in fact, but minimal minuscule dots, like points that by their multitude would recreate on the canvas the experience of seeing nature, bathing in light (*Pointillism*). A painting was technically speaking constructed like a machine, the implementation of a few inevitable laws of nature. Science, Seurat would hold, is more than an individual hobby, so is art. He intended art to grow beyond what he saw as the accidental intuitions of a Monet or Renoir, beyond the haphazard personal touch, and toward the structural monumentality of architecture. Beauty, he thought, could be free from chance and instincts; it could be certain as science. Only then art would find back the grandeur of old. And he thought of Egyptian murals, he imagined Greek statuary or Byzantine mosaics. He dared canvases of monumental size in which the solid pointillist manner was in colorful harmony with a strangely frozen composition of bustling actual life. It was both modern and timeless. It had a quality of antiquity, not copied, as the Academy taught, but discovered in its very reality.

Seurat was not alone in his search of a symbolic antiquity through modern reality; or, to put it in another way, in his search of the naïve sincerity that seemed to have nourished old art. It could be said to be the common factor of a great number of very talented artists, independent from each other, exponents of different national cultures, and all developing a personal style to realize it. We have given to this idealistic approach to art the name of Symbolism. Art and poetry went hand in hand. All agree in a skeptical or pessimistic attitude towards the progress made in science and politics, in industrialization and mechanization. In their minds and hands art would combat omnipresent materialism, while glorifying the immaterial spirit as the essential value. Amidst countless valuable artists, the sculptor Auguste Rodin may be considered *primus inter pares,* the artist of his age according to many. His figures, often nudes, and this is typical for Symbolism, have the physical beauty of Greek athletes, the fervor of gothic martyrs, and the melancholic air of Michelangelo's slaves, but they possess the utter tension, even anxiety, of modern times. Splendid bodies of women or men are inhabited by restless minds, sowing a tragic spleen. Hidden in the flesh there is a soul that aspires to a higher reality; that strives to escape from the bond with the earth. Nothing symbolizes this lust for spirituality better than the desire for love; uncontrollable sexual attraction is the symbol of man's metaphysical destiny. It is moreover the symbol of the fundamental forces that govern both matter and life in their origin or principle, suffering from their separation from divinity. Love is the need for unification and its metaphor is the kiss. Rodin's *Kiss* is probably the most famous one in history. The kiss became a favorite theme in art in these years around 1900. How rare it had been before! How many tried now, like Aubrey Beardsley, or Ferdinand Hodler, beautifully! But the other most famous *Kiss* is the one painted, in many versions, by the Austrian Symbolist Gustav Klimt. Those kisses are no light stroking of thoughtless lips. Klimt's *Kiss to the World* found his justification in the epic wording of the poet Friedrich Schiller, who in his turn inspired Beethoven to his Ninth Symphony: *"Alle Menschen werden Brüder".* It dodged the Vienna of Gustav Mahler and Arnold Schönberg into the focus of new art. Rodin's *Kiss* came from the *Gates of Hell*, his never finished masterpiece inspired by Dante's *Inferno.* According to the poet, the couple, trespassing against the laws of marriage, was killed in the very moment of love (by the jealous husband). Kiss of love, kiss of death. Inseparable *Eros* and *Thanatos* are a characteristic theme for the pessimistic world view of Symbolist artists. *Death and the Maiden* is a variation on this ancient dark theme, worked out anew by Edvard Munch, for instance, and Egon Schiele.

Pessimism was not the world view of Vincent van Gogh, the Dutch artist, who in spite of a failing career, became probably the most famous of all those who joined the Paris school. His artistic personality strove for a very different ideal. The story of his life is well known; it offered the world a model of the artist, which still finds wide recognition as the truest: the misunderstood genius. He was the one who never sold a drawing in his lifetime and whose works are now the top treasures of museums. Only mention, to anyone you know, the *Sunflowers, Irises* or *Potato Eaters*. Although this was in part his fate, it was not how he saw himself or how he saw the sense of art. For him art was a celebration of life and the artist was there to make this come true.

This is the paradox: Rodin was the acknowledged sculptor of his time, rich and honored by artists and social elite, applauded by the public, during a long life; his art is pessimist, suffering, fatalist. Van Gogh was hardly recognized as an artist at all, without a dime in his pocket and sick always, in body and mind, rejected by society, interned and suicidal, dying as a young man, exhausted and desolate; but his art is optimist, determined, a conquest of life and the joy in nature. So we should never reduce art to the biography of an artist.

For Vincent (as he liked to be known, not Van Gogh), objective observation, in-depth knowledge and honest rendering of nature was the basis of art. If that speaks to you, Vincent is your man. He has been faithful to nature up to his last painting. But he also realized that nature is not the same to everyone. It is colored by the inner life of the person who observes it. By personality. Art is the interaction between a personality and life's experience. Art shows life faithfully, though formatted by a unique character. This is what Vincent had learned from his favorite authors and artists. He himself had never considered becoming an artist, until he was far in his twenties. He was a passionate reader, knew his moderns well, Victor Hugo, Charles Dickens, Emile Zola, and might have thought of a career as a writer for himself. His image of art was on the contrary conservative, influenced by the Dutch seventeenth century and the older masters of his own century, Delacroix, Millet, Israëls. When he became a painter he had to make up for these lacunae, but he never forgot, and he worked hard to make his art equal to the old masters; his backwardness became finally an advantage.

Speaking about authors and artists, he liked them when they aroused in him emotions. The more he understood art and life, the more he identified his own life with art. In the end this would be fatal for him personally, but not before he had opened a new path to art. He was an emotional man. So his art would be emotional. How to translate emotion to pictorial form? He trained his hand and his eye. Because the emotion that is *in us*, is to be found and studied *out there*. There his hand gained the traits of a dynamic and willful character. The eye also responds to color and form according to personality. In the first years of his career, Vincent painted very dark scenes, in which the slightest color segment would gain the emotional (and of course symbolic) impact of a candle in the night. Later, in Paris, he joined the Impressionist movement, a total conversion, because it shunned the dark completely from its palette, seeing colors only in full sunlight. His colors changed, all to his joy, not his dynamic brush, the essence of his style. The character of his brush strokes, translating his personality and emotions, continued to serve the character of his subjects. When finally he lived alone in the South of France he freed himself from the past and from the presence and the pressure of the art world. He brought together the disparate elements of his discoveries and laid down the foundations of a new style, the originality of which is expression of personal (inner) experience by purely pictorial means. In three liberating steps: 1) the brush strokes, he sets them free; they run on the canvas like happy children, entrusting to the paint the rhythm of his emotional vivacity. 2) The colors, he sets them free; purified and simplified, held in hand by the rules of complementarity and contrast, they obey to pictorial logic alone which is the visual emotion itself, boldly challenging suffocating conventions. 3) Meaning and outreach, he sets them free. Speaking as to a world he will not see, he delivers a symbolic image of the world in the form of a personal style and makes it universal.

The experience finds direct incarnation in paint, and however simple it may be, a flower, a tree, a moon, a butterfly, it stands out unique like a human being.

To enhance emotion the painter submitted himself (not always quite voluntarily) to extreme situations, characterized by poverty, hunger, insomnia, long hikes, solitude, bad health, bad temper, and pipe tobacco.

An interesting component of extreme experience was the fact that Vincent van Gogh in his last year and a half suffered from attacks of mental disorder. Let us be very aware here: when he suffered from these long-lasting, violent attacks, he did not paint, and when he painted he did not suffer from attacks, but was clear in his mind and dominated his subject. His art is not the blueprint of his disease; on the contrary. However, Vincent was not an ordinary man, and it is legitimate to point to connections between his pathology, his sour life (and death), and his emotional art. Disease and art are never only physiological and psychological but also social facts. First of all, in all centuries artists have been accused (or excused) for socially improper or non-adapted behavior. The crazy artist, or the mentally suffering one, was commonplace since the Renaissance (when depression was called melancholy). However, in the nineteenth century the social isolation of the artist and the growing split between art and public, resulting in growing economic insecurity and diminishing public support for the artist, had aggravated the situation. More and more the public believed that art was for the sake of the artists alone, and the artists believed that it was their lonely affair. Art was looked upon as the style of an artist; an artist, in consequence, as someone looking for a style. This, the public would buy; or much more often, not buy. Vincent's life was a one-man war against this state of affairs. His painting (and writing) was a courageous struggle for art as comfort for all, a profoundly joyous action against a grim reality. He adopted the strategy that, in order to be heard by the almost deaf, a man must sometimes shout out loud, and to be seen from far, like blossoming trees in the spring, art must simplify its forms and intensify its colors without fear of excess. This is what will be called expressionism. Against all odds, Vincent has won more than one battle, however sick his carcass. He did change a corner of art.

Since his towering performance, the world reaches out to art as the expression of inner conditions: emotional, unconventional, personal. The soul of an art work comes from within. Art is what has to come out. Surprisingly, the public sees art often as the outlet for a sad or even sick constitution. The first 25 to 50 years after Vincent's death, and before he was recognized as the father of Expressionism, his art was commonly commented upon as the outcome of a mad mind. As if his mental disease was the seed of his relative artistic success. That is an error. It is rather true, however, that our society projects its own social disorders onto art, and its psychological problems to its artists. That explains why art expresses, through the artist's psyche, the inner tensions of the society. Many artists are unprepared to carry this weight. And the society is uneasy about this reminder of a reality it produces itself. The world's emotive reactions during a century to Vincent's life and death are exemplary in this context.

Before the wider public did so, artists recognized the originality of Vincent's approach to brushwork and color intensity as an expression of a total commitment to art. Particularly in the northern part of Europe his example provoked strong echoes. Edvard Munch combined Symbolism and expressive freedom in a personal way before even the end of the century. In Austria several followers of Klimt in his Secession group adopted a similar form of Expressionist Symbolism (my term), in particular Oskar Kokoschka and Egon Schiele. Now we are in a new century and we find groups of young artists in Germany, where the term Expressionism will be coined, notably *Die Brücke* (The Bridge) in Dresden and *Der Blaue Reiter* (The Blue Rider) in Munich. In Paris, painters grouped under the name of the *Fauves*, like Henri Matisse and André Derain owed much to Vincent's liberating and bold flattening of the picture space, as did after World War I Chaim Soutine to his impasto and free brushwork. From then on the presence of Expressionist's aesthetics has only won ground, towards almost entire submersion of the painter's body in the painting that represents him or her.

Let me finish with a note. Perhaps the quasi mythological proportions Vincent's life story assumed during those decades have accelerated the acceptance of a social phenomenon of our time, without even speaking of the vast field of art therapy: art as the only possible form of communication many *outcasts* entertain with the community. Works by prisoners, mentally ill, and weirdoes of all feathers have been given the name of *Art Brut* by the expressionist Jean Dubuffet. His collection is the core of the fast-growing treasure of a uniquely moving museum in Lausanne, Switzerland.

MAJOR WORKS AND MONUMENTS

Austria, Vienna, Österreichische Galerie Belvedere, Egon Schiele, *The Embrace*

Austria, Vienna, Secession Building, Gustav Klimt, *Beethoven Frieze*

Austria, Vienna, Österreichische Galerie Belvedere, Gustav Klimt, *The Kiss*

France, Paris, Musée d'Orsay, Paul Signac, *Portrait of the Art Critic Félix Fénéon*

France, Paris, Musée Rodin, Auguste Rodin, *The Kiss*

France, Paris, Musée Rodin, Auguste Rodin, *The Thinker*

France, Paris, Musée Rodin, Camille Claudel, *The Age of Maturity*

Germany, Berlin, Alte Nationalgalerie, Caspar David Friedrich, *The Monk by the Sea*

Germany, Berlin, Brücke Museum, Ernst Ludwig Kirchner, *Nude Reclining before Mirror*

Germany, Munich, Neue Pinakothek, Vincent van Gogh, *Sunflowers in a Vase*

Great Britain, London, Tate Gallery, Joseph Mallord William Turner, *Snow Storm, Steam-Boat off a Harbour's Mouth*

Greece, Collection Niarchos, Vincent van Gogh, *Self-portrait with Bandaged Ear and Pipe*

Netherlands, Amsterdam, Vincent van Gogh Museum, Paul Gauguin, *Portrait of Vincent Painting Sunflowers*

Netherlands, Amsterdam, Vincent van Gogh Museum, Vincent van Gogh, *The Potato Eaters*

Netherlands, Otterlo, Museum Kröller-Müller, Georges Seurat, *Le Chahut*

Norway, Oslo, National Gallery, Edvard Munch, *The Scream*

Switzerland, Basel, Kunstmuseum, Oskar Kokoschka, *The Tempest* or *The Bride of the Wind*

USA, Chicago, IL, Art Institute, Georges Seurat, *A Sunday Afternoon on the Isle La Grand-Jatte*

USA, New York, NY, Museum of Modern Art, Vincent van Gogh, *Starry Night*

USA, New York, NY, Neue Galerie, Gustav Klimt, *Portrait of Adele Bloch-Bauer*

USA, Minneapolis, MN, Walker Art Center, Franz Marc, *The Large Blue Horses*

30. **Art as Freedom**

MODERNISM   **GAUGUIN - PICASSO**   **1880 – 1975**

One of the more exciting secrets or attractions of any artwork is that it encompasses desires that smolder in us too, and one of them is freedom. Freedom is the great business of our time. Art, always helpful, fulfills that *fantasy* with the public in the person of the artist, who can do whatever he or she likes: free from financial and moral restraints, free from bosses and patrons (and family!), free to wake up late and dream during work, free from psychological blockage, social hierarchy, and physical disadvantages. Not all at the time, please! Free to be oneself, with one's own job, to live the life one wishes. We visit museums on free days, teach art as free expression (compared to mathematics or foreign language!), and we feel free to critique any art piece in the world, be it the *Mona Lisa*. Pure fantasies turning easily into frustration leading to disdain and censure. But still, art awakens our desire or nostalgia of freedom.

No one understood better than Pablo Picasso the urge for freedom that as an underground river feeds our art appreciation. The twentieth century has venerated him as the free man *par excellence,* and with him all the workers in his trade. Maybe because the twentieth century knew so well what freedom was, since it combated it so bloodily, so cruelly, so efficiently? Communism, Fascism, National-Socialism, Racism, everybody knows the list.
The nineteenth century had set the tone. Capitalism, Imperialism, Colonialism... everybody knows. Everybody knows not how the arts in that century had developed as a constant struggle for liberation,

technical and institutional, mental and moral. To stay in France, quite dominating in the visual arts, and to stay in the arts, we see how Delacroix *liberates* painting from the academic handling of the brush, Courbet from academic subject matter, Manet from academic conservatism, Monet from academic exhibit monopoly... The *Académie des Beaux-Arts* was their *bête noire,* and with reason. When the Academy finally had to retreat, art seemed synonymous with a search for freedom against oppression, and not only of brushstrokes. The art scene developed in the Parisian neighborhoods Montmartre and Montparnasse, where dancing parties, bars, cabarets and brothels replaced what the Church was in the Middle Ages and the Court in classical times. After liberation from the tyranny of the school, art sought freedom from social pressure and control. The changing role of women illustrates it. Not only had their number as artists begun to grow, when the institutions didn't even recognize them. They were more than ever the major subject in figure painting and sculpture. Moreover, they played a role on the foreground in the very coming of modern art. From passive they became active. They were still the prominent models, but not anonymous or ideal, now real and known by name. The scandal in 1865 around *Olympia* was so great because the people in the public *knew* the model or thought they did and Manet had done nothing to prevent them from thinking that, on the contrary. Models for painters had traditionally been prostitutes or considered as such. Now Victorine Meurent, known as an *élégante*, modeled for a prostitute in the painting. Her nakedness *was* disturbing, wasn't it? This was really her, looking without shame at... you. Many taboos were broken here, but one was that of a woman taking possession of her body. Speaking about freedom! Victorine was in real life a painter and therefore befriended with painters. It was the case of another model of Manet, Berthe Morisot, painter and friend also of Mary Cassatt, the American painter and etcher, dedicated from the start to the cause of the Impressionists. Both have left a magnificent oeuvre. As did Suzanne Valadon, who started as a model for Edgar Degas, Henri de Toulouse-Lautrec, Pierre Puvis de Chavanne, Auguste Renoir, to name a few and became one of the most prominent painters of Paris in the new century. Even more well-known is the case of Camille Claudel, model and friend of Auguste Rodin. Art was for courageous and talented women a zone of relative freedom from suffocating social conventions. Sadly enough they also discovered that freedom was not the same as a free lunch and that the art world was still under the law of the jungle. Camille learned this when her relation with Rodin was broken off. Like many women she became trapped between the unforgiving worlds of art and conservative society. Her artistic genius would suffer from psychological unbalance and finally be imprisoned for life in mental asylums.

Many artists, not only women, who had chosen for the freedom of art, came in violent collision with the conservative society and more particularly with the iron laws of the art market. Vincent van Gogh's example is extreme, who sold only one painting in his life, and that for half the price. But all his friends were in financial trouble. Paul Gauguin, the strongest character between them and a visionary artist who declared himself a savage, drew the logical but radical conclusion: leave this sick society. Leave Paris. His first choice as a place to live was Brittany, a rural part of France, where ancient traditions seemed still intact. The definitive step was taken in 1891, when he sailed to the Pacific Tahiti islands. There he'd live on, he thought, like a new Adam in a new Eden, painting paradise. Here, too, reality proved to be a different story and Gauguin died already in 1903 from exhaustion, poisoning, and diseases, on the way even to prison. Nonetheless, we fall under the spell of his powerful quest for freedom.

Pablo Picasso did. Spanish born, the young man lived in Paris then, the life not of an exile but of a Bohemian, between brothel and circus, poverty and hard work, earning him a growing reputation. More than by Gauguin's self-styled life, he was impressed by the artistic harvest of that howl for freedom. This painter had been able to translate his hatred of the decadent European culture into suggestive imagery of savage beauty. In flat zones of blinding colors he had set up a true monument to the exotic dream of humanity, all in subconscious mystery and symbolism borne by immediate evidence. Picasso understood perfectly. Though exceptionally gifted, he had not yet an exceptional role in Paris. He had his "style" (the *Blue Period*) and followed closely the daring avant-garde. He was noted for his capacity of picking the best artists, seizing their style and staying himself. So with Toulouse-Lautrec, Van Gogh, Matisse, Derain. This eventually introduced him to an important discovery, in the line of Gauguin's initiations: real works from Polynesia and Africa. His favorites were face masks of the Chokwe people, sculptures on show in the museum of ethnography, not of art. In the same years around 1905 he discovered the audacious last works of the last Post-Impressionist, radical and unsuccessful Paul Cézanne, who died in 1906.

Like Seurat, Van Gogh and Gauguin, Paul Cézanne had been, earlier in his career, a convinced Impressionist, but he too had deemed it necessary to free himself from this still new style. It was for him too loose, to fluffy, to fast a manner of painting to be a real substitute for classic art. He retired voluntarily into the south of France, where he was from, and during twenty years of self-imposed isolation he reestablished the very process of painting, concentrating on composition, simplifying the basic means of brush and color application, building an image not imitating nature but parallel to nature. He was strongly attached to concrete subject matter, in still-life, landscape (*"Mountain Sainte-Victoire"*), portrait and figure ("*Bathers*"), but not as a narrative. As a visual adventure, one might say, or an elementary reconstruction of our visual activity. Art now happened entirely on the canvas, or in us, in our brain, while the relation to the visual world was simplified to functions like equilibrium, weight, structure, geometric relationships, at the expense of perspective and illusion. His approach opened the way to art as an autonomous construction of visual experiences on the canvas.

In 1906-07 Pablo Picasso drew the conclusions of his synthetic understanding of the mask, of Gauguin and of Cézanne and he painted a vast canvas *Les Demoiselles d'Avignon*. It was the terminal step in the evolution of Western art that had started with Courbet et Manet; it was the starting point of a new era, Modernism. The work liberated Western-European painting definitely from its most typical attribute: linear perspective with the single viewpoint. It is so easy to pen down those words, but imagine the difficulty when you realize that all Western thinking and seeing was based on it (and still is in everyday life). It was, indeed, the outcome of a colossal effort by Picasso. And it is rare that a major change in culture can be pinned down so precisely to one work. In fact, the canvas didn't have any impact at all, it was not seen. Even Picasso couldn't comprehend or oversee the vast sense of what his hands and eyes had wrought, let alone the consequences. He couldn't finish it completely. He folded it under his bed, waited and showed it to almost none. The world needed a moment to digest. Picasso used this time to work on smaller formats first, in still-life, landscape and portrait, to analyze his achievement and underwrite his own development before offering it to the public.

Fortunately, he was not alone; which proves once more that the world was ready, though someone had to tear the curtain.

There was Georges Braque, equally stimulated by his discovery of Cézanne; he had started a very similar research as Picasso, in the same time on the same subjects: landscape, still-life, portraits. Pushed by camaraderie and competition, the two friends rivaled in boldness and lucidity and banned from the canvas the underlying idea of the "window on the world," the visual illusion, or the Renaissance mirror. Painting became what it actually is: two-dimensional, flat forms on a flat support. There was still a real object as model, a jug, a guitar, a pipe, a face or a view. But as a subject in the painting or drawing it was broken up in separate elements and rebuilt as a composite of precious little blocks of volume and color, treated individually, and quasi monochromatically. That composition, and not a simulacrum of space, must provoke the pictorial unity on the canvas. The new style was coined Cubism and was to art what Einstein's theories were to physics. Published in the same years, artists and physicians chained the notion of Time to the notion of Space, and symbolically alluded to it as the fourth dimension. And they experienced the same opposition from the public.

Who would want to see and join Braque's and Picasso's almost excessive freedom? This is the question; or rather the enigma. Art doesn't exist without a public. Who would pay money for such an unprofitable looking research? This honor comes to a German art dealer in Paris, Daniel-Henry Kahnweiler, a passionate amateur of daring innovative art and daring innovative artists. He first opened the doors of his gallery for a show of Georges Braque in 1908, and the idea of cubes was critically launched. From then on he showed Picasso and Braque regularly. In a very small circle the new art was accepted, and the two painters were free to continue their campaign.

In 1911 painting was ripe for the last blow: the guillotine for the king of all media, oil. Braque and Picasso freed art from the constraint of oil on canvas and pencil on paper. They stuck other materials to the flat surface of the canvas. Wallpaper, a drawing, oil-cloth, newspaper, sand: a *collage.* We should situate here the germ of the technique we call mixed media. Pictures, from realistic (or *copying reality)*, were becoming real, that is, principally matter. Here is where twentieth century art was definitely launched.

From that multiple stroke of genius on, Picasso unfurled his unrivaled talents during 60 more years. Very soon he showed the real extent of his freedom, this time shocking not the general public, but his art brothers. Cubism had hardly received a beginning of recognition, and Picasso seemed to abandon it, returning to painting like Ingres and to drawing like Raphael. It was decried as a blunt betrayal of the cause of modernism. But the artist simply stated that nobody could reduce him to a style; that he could handle more than one at the time. He *was* his style. Picasso went his way; resisting classification. He evolved above the laws, artistic and social. Rarely a man has been so admired and so scorned. His energy, originality and prolificacy became legendary. His artistic courage was an example for all artists of his generation. His show of independence became the rule for all: an artist always freed the arts from one law or another. Liberation was the law.

Picasso became the icon of modern art. This now was far from a compliment in the mouth of almost all, the entire Western society that is, stretching from Moscow over Munich and Madrid to Mississippi. Modern art became the paradigm of decadence, anarchy, and nihilism in the eyes of the multitude and of many a leader, who hit back with unseen vehemence. The arts of the October Revolution, extraordinary phenomenon in terms of avant-garde, especially Constructivism, were soon strictly forbidden in the communist Soviet Union and the artists were killed, banished to

Siberia, forced into the Party or into exile. In Nazi Germany *Degenerate Art* exhibits traveled the country; modern art museums were closed; their treasures were sold to Swiss banks or to Jews who were later robbed and killed to have the works sold a second time; the artists were sent to the camps or forced to join the party or go into exile. In America those modern arts had hardly come yet, they were still seen as European extravaganza; or as Mexican impertinence: Diego Riviera's master fresco *Man at the Cross Roads* in the Rockefeller Center was destroyed on Nelson Rockefellers own order when Lenin's portrait had been included in the composition. On the other hand, exiled artists found in America a hospitable new home.

These were terrible times that as never before tried to kill the living arts.

But, although artists are vulnerable, the arts are invincible. And even if the ongoing specialization of the society had isolated them from the public, they were not less the spirit of its civilization. Its invisible backbone. A visible battle took place on the grounds of the Universal Exhibition in Paris, 1937. Pablo Picasso represented Spain, his fatherland, plunged in a most devastating Civil War. He was the one who could symbolically resist General Franco's army, assisted by Hitler's airplanes and bombs. In the modest Spanish pavilion, designed by Josep Luis Sert, surrounded by Joan Miró and Salvador Dali, all living in Paris, Picasso delivered the strongest artistic feat of the century. In the middle of the raging propaganda fight between Nazis, Fascists and Communists, the artist showed in the strongest Modernist style the reality of human suffering caused by unfree men. *Guernica, oil on canvas, 11'5½" x 25'5¾"*. With one masterstroke and forever Picasso underscored that the quest for freedom by the arts was the highly symbolical search of social, psychological, and even physical freedom of civilization itself.

MAJOR WORKS AND MONUMENTS

Denmark, Copenhagen, Ordrupgaard Collection, Berthe Morisot, *Portrait of Madame Hubbard*

France, Paris, Musée Picasso, Pablo Picasso, *Still Life with Chair-Caning*

France, Paris, Musée National d'Art Moderne, Centre Georges Pompidou, Georges Braque, *Still Life with Violin, Pipe, and « Le Quotidien »*

France, Paris, Musée National d'Art Moderne, Centre Georges Pompidou, Suzanne Valadon, *The Blue Room*

Great Britain, Edinburgh, National Museum of Scotland, Paul Gauguin, *A Vision after the Sermon, Jacob Wrestling with the Angel*

Mexico, Mexico City, Palacio de Bellas Artes, Diego Rivera, *Man, Controller of the Universe* (originally USA, New York, NY, Rockefeller Center, Diego Rivera, *Man at the Crossroads*)

Russia, Moscow, State Tretyakow Gallery, Marc Chagall, *Introduction to the Jewish Theatre*

Russia, St Petersburg, Hermitage Museum, Paul Gauguin, *Pastorales Tahitiennes*

Spain, Madrid, Centro de Arte Reina Sofia, Pablo Picasso, *Guernica*

Switzerland, Bern, Kunstmuseum, Georges Braque, *Houses at L'Estaque*

Switzerland, Zurich, E. G. Bührle Foundation, Paul Cézanne, *Self-portrait with Palette*

USA, Boston, MA, Museum of Fine Arts, Paul Gauguin, *Where Are We From? What Are We? Where Are We Going?*

USA, Cambridge, MA, Fogg Art Museum, Max Beckmann, *The Actors*

USA, Chicago, Art Institute, Pablo Picasso, *Portrait of Kahnweiler*

USA, Merion, PA, Barnes Foundation, Paul Cézanne, *Montagne Sainte-Victoire*

USA, New York, NY, Guggenheim Museum, Georges Braque, *Violin and Palette*

USA, New York, NY, Museum of Modern Art, Pablo Picasso, *Les Demoiselles d'Avignon*

USA, Philadelphia, PA, Museum of Art, Mary Cassatt, *Woman with a Pearl Necklace in a Loge*

USA, Philadelphia, PA, Museum of Art, Paul Cézanne, *The Large Bathers*

USA, Philadelphia, PA, Museum of Art, Salvador Dali, *Premonition of Civil War*

31. **Art as Color and Line**

MODERNISM   **KANDINSKY - BAUHAUS**   **1900 - 75**

Picasso is action, Kandinsky is contemplation. One cannot learn from the Spaniard, or it would be courage, character, and confidence. From the Russian, in every square inch he touched, one learns about painting. Pablo is the summit of European individualism; Wassily reconciles you with the universe. The one is all about women, war, work, the world; the other about red, blue, and green. Picasso has rehabilitated matter, Kandinsky the mind. They are the two poles between which the arts have evolved until deep into the twentieth century, each with an irresistible force of attraction.

Pablo Picasso was a realist. That is, a painting, a sculpture, a print, always generated from actual objects or situations, nudes, flowers, paintings, doves, that kept their presence in the paint, clay, or whatever other medium. He saw a bull's head in a bike seat and handlebars. Or a baboon's in a car toy. However often he changed his "style" (Symbolist, Cubist, Classical, Surrealist, Expressionist, etc.) we tell his *hand* from far, his particular energy, his signature. He never explained his method, because he had no method, other than his hand and hawk's eye. Reality was what intrigued him and moved him; to capture that emotion was his mission, from his earliest works to his last. And even in his most complex Cubist constructions, the figure is the starting point and the goal of his enterprise, be it a lover or a glass of wine. When he is quoted in words, it is in the form of aphorisms, gems of intelligence that explain nothing but his genius (*"I don't search, I find"*).

Wassily Kandinsky, on the contrary, was an idealist. His images are visualized movements of the mind, borne from inner necessity, and their names are concepts, poetic or musical performances, *prophecies* he would almost claim, drawn from his contagious imagination. *The Blue Rider, Painting with Black Arch, The Garden of Love, Lyrical.* He was proud to write books and articles. He explained in beautiful language and well-chosen similes his spiritual world view and the prominent role of the arts in our civilization. He was a teacher to the marrow of his bones. His ideals were *synesthetic,* which means sensations in one field of art provoke reactions in another and in the end influence all human activity.

Kandinsky started his career as an artist late and not in his beloved hometown Moscow, but in art active Munich, Germany. He passionately loved myths and music. His pressing quest was how painting could attain the mystery of tales and the emotion of tunes. And considering that music had evolved from accompanying words to pure tone, he knew that the time had come for painting to evolve from telling a story to touching directly the heart. Color was the instrument, and its distribution on the canvas was to provoke our spontaneous reaction.

It was natural that one day Wassily Kandinsky was going to do away with figurative subject matter. But again: how easy to say and how hard to do. The enormous impact a subject used to have on the viewer's mind should not be lost, but taken care of by pure color. The risk was that painting would fall back on decorative patterning. For years the very good painter he was struggled with the problem. He had strong support from friends, including Gabriele Münter, Franz Marc, August Macke, Alexej Jawlensky and Paul Klee with whom he founded a movement, *Der Blaue Reiter*, expressionist in spirit, and published an almanac (magazine) with the same name. In it he unfolded his ideas, which run faster than his practice (which is evidence of his honesty and craftsmanship). Not until after 1910 his figures began to dissolve step by step into their colors and assume pure form some years later. Abstract art was born, in long labor and pain; but a beautiful child it was. Kandinsky is generally held for its father, although there are other pretenders, Alfred Kubin, for instance, or Robert Delaunay. But Kandinsky surely gave it the best care. *Abstract* was the name given to the child that would grow into the outstanding hero of the twentieth-century legacy. *Abstract* was the word the common people chose, when they still held modern art for utterly revolutionary. It was never quite satisfactory, but what is in a name? Non-figurative, non-representational, objective, also non-objective, many other names were invented from that time on, by painters and critics; until *abstract* was nothing striking anymore, three generations later. Kandinsky himself had more *musical* appellations for his offspring: compositions, improvisations.

Visual art now had been taken down to its most bare formula. What had started with the Impressionists (*Art is what sees the Eye*) had been brought to its conclusion (*the Eye sees only Color and Line*). Although the wider public stayed hostile or indifferent, it seemed for long the only and inescapable destiny of the arts. Abstract became another word for modern or contemporary. Great artists drew immediately the logical consequences from these premises and forged bold theories on these foundations, mixing rationality and contemporary mystique: Kazimir Malewich, who proposed Suprematism from 1915 on and painted the ultimate icon *White on White*, 1918; Piet Mondrian, who founded *De Stijl,* 1917, a radical art magazine in which he explained his creeds, while composing pure balance between blue, red, yellow and white rectangles in black lining. The larger public showed even more contempt now.

The art of painting thus being reduced to a degree close to zero, it did not disappear, which some foresaw. On the contrary, forced to concentrate on its very essentials, it could begin to radiate on new fields of activity, and it is from there that its influence on general culture would finally be revived. Since some fifty years the arts and the crafts had started to invert a tendency that during several centuries had made them grow apart. William Morris must be mentioned as the pioneer in Great Britain of the *Arts and Crafts* movement which preached the rebirth of beauty for functional objects in a machine obsessed age. Its aesthetics was originally a form of nostalgia for the Middle Ages with its hand produced objects, but developed into a recognizable style based on observation of nature, graphic and decorative, using noble materials crafted by expert hands. Towards the end of the century the crafts in many countries of Europe and America had exponentially grown in number and creative invention, competing overtly with the arts in spirituality and idealism. A distinctive language of form had come into being the characteristics of which were grounded in the stylized celebration of organic forms, particularly botanic, in constant growth and sweeping health. To this all the materials, whatever their nature, had to conform: iron, wood, glass and cement. The idea of *total art* (*Gesamtkunstwerk*) belonged to it, in which all the arts and crafts without precedence over each other combined in synthetic enterprises, from architecture to furniture, book design and lamp poles, metro stations and theater posters, including window decoration, wall paper, painting, ceramic tiles, stucco reliefs and what not else... Called Art Nouveau or Jugendstil in most languages, it had decorative affinities with Symbolism, and with oriental taste. It fitted the demands of visibility in the fast growing cities in many corners of the continent before World War One, and even more so in the USA. In Paris the architect Hector Guimard gives elegant form to the new metro stations, in Vienna Otto Wagner does the same. In Chicago we should mention groundbreaking works by the father of great American architecture, Louis Sullivan, and the early works of his successor, Frank Lloyd Wright. With ever better craftsmanship, colorful and distinguished, refined and costly, the Art Nouveau style does enliven monotonous neighborhoods that preceded it, and is responsible for many a luxury setting in wealthy interiors. Its most famous exponent and definitely an incorrigible utopist and experimenter, was the Barcelona architect Antonio Gaudí. He has left the most astounding urban landmarks to the proud capital of Catalonia, an undeniable milestone in the history of architecture.

As fast as the movement had spread, though, as fast it lost momentum. Uncontrolled urban expansion before and after WWI, and the growing complexity of planned urbanism, asked for more radical and rational solutions in architecture than the purely aesthetic ones put forward by Art Nouveau. The historic step was set by the *Bauhaus*, from 1919 till 1933, a school founded in Weimar, Germany, by the architect Walter Gropius; later it moved to Dessau. It is here where modern design was invented. The modest-size school of applied arts and architecture assumed the concept of *total art*, which ignores traditional hierarchical differences between the arts and the crafts. The principles of the philosophy of progress, such as rationalism, functionalism, abstract patterns and mass production, were to be transferred to the forms of new industrial articles, furniture, graphic design, typography, and architecture. The ideas of Suprematism, Constructivism and De Stijl entered very naturally in the curriculum.

In this school and this ambiance Wassily Kandinsky was for many years the professor of form and color, core courses all students would follow. Here his insights in the abstract aesthetics of color and line were put to the test in the sphere of practical applications; here they were transmitted to a talented new generation of designers. An excellent team of professors, strong individualities from various countries and future celebrities in their specialty, would develop for the (so-called) minor arts many a precept underlying the painter's abstract work. And from the feed-back Kandinsky took his own painting deeper into the century. From this interaction the Bauhaus initiated the layout and design of modernity, from advertisement and film to skyscrapers and airplanes.

Alas, we are in Germany in the thirties. Every one of the Bauhaus principles, from its educational methods to its concrete results, was a thorn in the eye of the Nazi party. When it came to power, one of its first deeds in government was to destroy the school (in the same blow they destroyed Kandinsky's first abstract compositions, cultural milestones) and the professors had to run for their lives. The irony of the story is that by its dismantlement, the Nazis spread the seeds of the ideas that after their fall would reshape the world. Many of its teachers, prosecuted in Germany, were warmly received in the United States. The influence of the Bauhaus would be strong there. The architects Walter Gropius and Marcel Breuer reorganized the Harvard University School of Design. The painter and photographer László Moholy-Nagy was in 1937 the first director of the "New Bauhaus" in Chicago (now the IIT Institute of Design). Its most famous teacher there would be the architect Ludwig Mies van der Rohe. Many of America's schools of art and design, architecture, and technology were based on Bauhaus ideas and curriculum. A special mention should go however to Black Mountain College, NC. A radical, idealistic and coherent

Bauhaus experience went on there from 1933 to 1957 under the inspired lead of Josef Albers. The practice of *synesthesia* was successfully pursued, when the great talents of America, still young but future stars (such as John Cage for music, Merce Cunningham for dance, Buckminster Fuller for architecture, Willem de Kooning for painting) taught at the one and unique school of higher learning, where the arts were the center of the curriculum.

Kandinsky's mark on the arts has finally been as great as Picasso's, whose individual approach came in the velvet grip of the art market. But Picasso was famous, a hero. Kandinsky was not, rather a victim; he was chased from Germany in 1933. Too old to leave the continent (but not to paint like a master) he lived a modest life in Paris, where he died in 1944, mourned by a few art lovers alone.

MAJOR WORKS AND MONUMENTS

Josef Albers, *Interaction of Color* (color theory)
Wassily Kandinsky, *On the Spiritual in Art* (art theory)

Paul Klee, *Diaries* (reflections of an artist)
Kasimir Malewich, *Suprematism* (art theory)

Belgium, Brussels, Victor Horta, *House and Studio* (now Horta Museum)
Czech Republic, Prague, Mucha Museum, Alphonse Mucha, *Sarah Bernhardt Gismonda* (lithograph)
France, Paris, Musée du Petit Palais, Emile Gallé, *Vase Marguerite Gallé*

Great Britain, London, Tate Gallery, Josef Albers, *Homage to the Square*
Great Britain, London, Victoria & Albert Museum, William Morris, *Green Dining Room*
Netherlands, Amsterdam, Stedelijk Museum, Piet Mondrian, *Composition IV, with Red, Blue and Yellow*

Netherlands, Rotterdam, Museum Boymans-Van Beuningen, Wassily Kandinsky, *Lyrical (The Rider)*

Netherlands, The Hague, Gemeentemuseum, Theo van Doesburg, *Counter-Composition of Dissonances XVI*

Netherlands, The Hague, Gemeentemuseum, Piet Mondrian, *Victory Boogie-Woogie*

Russia, Moskow, State Tretyakov Gallery, Wassily Kandinsky, *Composition VII*

Russia, Moskow, State Tretyakov Gallery, Kasimir Malewich, *Black Square*

Russia, Saint Petersburg, Hermitage Museum, Wassily Kandinsky, *Composition VI*

Spain, Barcelona, Antonio Gaudi, arch., *Park Güell*

Switzerland, Basel, Kunstmuseum, Paul Klee, *Senecio*

Switzerland, Bern, Zentrum Paul Klee, Paul Klee, *Insula Dulcamara*

USA, Chicago, IL, Illinois Institute of Technology, Ludwig Mies van der Rohe, *Campus Master Plan*

USA, Chicago, IL, Louis Sullivan, *Carson, Pirie, Scott and Company Building* (now Louis Sullivan Center)

USA, Malibu, CA, J. Paul Getty Museum, László Moholy-Nogy, *Light-Space Modulator*

USA, New York, NY, Museum of Modern Art, Kasimir Malewich, *Suprematist Composition: White on White*

USA, Utica, NY, Munson Williams Proctor Arts Institute, Wassily Kandinsky, *Improvisation XXIII*

32. **Art as Nature**

ABSTRACT EXPRESSIONISM   POLLOCK – TAPIES   1940 – 80

Someone (a skeptic gallery owner) asked Jackson Pollock: "Why don't you draw after nature?"

And Pollock answered: "Because I *am* nature."

Pollock was making big pictures with nothing but dripping paint.

Nature in the (naïve) question refers to all you can see with your eyes and can draw with your hand. It was the vocabulary and pedagogy of the art academies worldwide. They imposed on their students to learn a technique, a craft, by copying relentlessly according to distinct methods on flat paper the three-dimensional objects of reality. They still do.

For Pollock nature was something else and had nothing to do with the arts. It was the pulsing rhythm of the universe, the creative and destructive forces of life, the forests and the rivers, and the mountains and the stars. Not art, please. It was the beating of his heart, the urge of his sex, the blood in his veins, the pain in his brain.

Jackson Pollock was born in 1912, the year when Kandinsky published his defense of abstraction through color *On the Spiritual in Art,* while Carl Gustav Jung traveled the United States and published *The Theory of Psychoanalysis.* This was the decade of the First World War, which signed, with never equaled blind devastation, the death of Europe's hegemony in the world. After this hecatomb no one could trust technical progress anymore. Artists declared the death of art. It seemed a reasonable claim. A group of poets and artists, called Dada, did its best to show that it was true, but soon appeared that it wasn't. It is impossible.

Art is in a sense society's immortal part. Artists can declare what they want, the society decides if there is art or not. And *what* it is. Marcel Duchamp understood this. And to show this, with bitter French irony, he submitted under a false name a urinal to a candid New York art show, only four years after the first modern art exhibition in America, the *Armory Show* of 1913. Not *made* by him, but *found*: a *ready-made*. To make it worse he named it *Fountain*. Not surprisingly, it was rejected. That was part of the artist's strategy. In the rejection was the recognition. Potential discussion, thought-provoking presence/absence: new critical jargon. Then the object was lost. Even better! The thing as such never counted. The *concept* did. From then on the *idea* of a urinal haunted the spirits for fifty years and became the central piece in the ongoing chess game between art and society. In America it became the most famous artwork of the last hundred years. In the year 2000 a highbrow art magazine asked its readers to choose *the* artwork of the past century, hence *the* artist. You know the answer already. Even a urinal is doomed to become spirit when it enters into art. Now four (?) art museums are proud to have purchased a *copy* (of a non-existing object). And Sherrie Levine, a conceptual artist, had an almost faithful copy made in *bronze*.

So Marcel Duchamp became a most influential artist without almost ever producing anything but...thought. Witty indeed, daring, prolific, consistent, necessary without doubt, contagious and even slightly desperate. This happened in the First World War, when his fatherland was fighting a battle for life or for death. He had fled to New York. Maybe, with the *Fountain,* cynicism entered into art. That was probably prophetic too.

In other words art didn't die; the society needed it more than ever. Dada became art. Anti-art became art. In the short years until the next war, European society reacted artistically with vigor.

Modigliani, Surrealism (with Dali, Miró, Ernst, Magritte...), Picasso, Chagall, Matisse, Derain, Mondrian and many others worked in Paris (where Claude Monet offered his masterpiece to his country: the *Nympheas* of the Orangerie); the Bauhaus artists, the Expressionists (Nolde, Schmidt-Rottluff, Heckel, Kirchner), Beckmann, Gross, Dix worked in Berlin and Munich; the Constructivists (Lissitzky, Tatlin, Pevsner, Rodchenko) in Moskow and Leningrad, to randomly name a few. All of them seemed to have put the First World War between brackets. But a Second World War announced itself. It would erase the illusions for good. There is no need to repeat the list of horrors of that war. In 1945 Europe, materially and morally, was on its back, exhausted.

How did art react this time? Did art react? It is, you will be surprised to learn, a question seldom raised. As if the public couldn't see and the art world refused to see. As if the split between society and art was consummated, and as if art had no voice anymore in important matters. Had it? It is far from easy to form an opinion in this case.

Anyway, art would not tell the story as realism would. That was the work of the photo journalists. Art's language of the age was that of abstraction, of Surrealism, of Expressionism, of collage and mixed media. There is where we have to lend our ear, and open our eye. To discover that the artists "simply" went further in breaking down the traditional view of art and the world. Apparently something was still wrong there; the work, started around 1900, was not finished. The strongest statements concerning our questioning came in the later fifties and sixties. Why so late? Realize that, after the war's end, the amplitude of the horrors came in at a slow pace, the genocide and the treason, the villains and the victims. People spread a veil of heroism over the common guilt. And how would *you* face an arsenal of nuclear bombs hanging in the air above your country, the probable battleground for a conflict between two aggressive powers? It was called the Cold War.

Do you want more? Well, Britain, France, the Netherlands, Portugal, Belgium, all these countries lost their age old colonies, often after bloody fighting and severe humiliation. On the other end of the planet China's path to communism was paved with massacres, while Japan licked its wounds after the ongoing trauma of Hiroshima. We shouldn't be surprised to see that some artists, realizing this state of the world, had stopped painting flowers in a vase, even though in a cubist manner. They "copied" another reality, the reality of violence, destruction, indifference, anguish and terror. Not consciously, not planned, not as a literal comment, that would be out of place (some artists, like Bernard Lorjou, tried to bring back this nineteenth century form of social engagement). No, artists work from their artist's intuition which may or may not fit in a "style" or "movement" that a gallery can sell with a smile. But seen from a certain height we can't escape from noticing a resemblance in spirit between art and a world in permanent war. How to represent or to express violence? How destruction? By attacking and destroying the very material of your trade. Here follow a few striking examples. Argentinian in Milan, Lucio Fontana slashed his canvases with a sharp knife, leaving gaping wounds, or he attacked them with a drill and left empty holes. Italian in Rome, Alberto Burri made large collages of old and worn (*Marshall Plan!*) sacks of torn burlap, with big dark holes in them, sometimes draped and stiffened by thick dry paint. Irishman in London, Francis Bacon was more respectful to his media, but not to the content: art threatened by art history; he visited the masters, examined their vital strength and it was as if he painted with their blood and marrow. Frenchman in Paris, Pierre Soulages decided to work exclusively in black paint or ink, condemning all other colors. Swiss in Paris, Alberto Giacometti let his bronze men en women grow thinner and thinner, their skin growing rougher and rougher, like the furrowed earth, resulting in eerie disproportioned bodies, walking bones, surprisingly not unreal, but dramatic. Elegant, too. Just as Fontana's slashed canvases, that he called *Concepts in Space,* definitely aesthetic. As the huge black canvases of Pierre Soulages, almost mystically introducing the nature of light. And as Francis Bacon's *Crucifixions* and *Popes,* terribly powerful, preceding sweeping portraits of friends and himself. We are tantalized. Can we say beautiful? Is the germ of construction inside destruction? These were great artists and their language was powerful, to the point, deep. People who visit the Antoni Tàpies Foundation in Barcelona say it is beautiful. It is the beauty of a battle field, of a factory abandoned since human memory, of a drug-stricken neighborhood. Tàpies was a teenager during the Spanish Civil War. In his art we recognize enduring destruction, the letting out of violence. Also energy and strength; the will and capacity to construct on ruins. See the traces of handwriting, the nail scratching and the recurrent signs, like in prehistoric grottos the mysterious presence of a human spirit, see the obsessive use of otherwise lost though broken human artefacts. Can we expect a better global image of the time? At least in Europe?

If Tàpies had had to answer to a question similar to the one put at the top of this chapter, he would have said: I *am* culture.

Which brings us back to Jackson Pollock and the USA.

With the First World War an important shift in Western civilization had set in. Its center of gravity moved to the United States. This cultural drift was confirmed in the nineteen forties by WWII and by the birth of Abstract Expressionism. In the first decades of the century excellent artists had come to the fore, photographers (Alfred Stieglitz, Edward Steichen), painters (Edward Hopper, Georgia O'Keeffe) and sculptors (Augustus Saint Gaudens, Frederic Remington). Now American art freed itself from the European shadow. With Jackson Pollock it stood in the sun.

European art since Kandinsky was expressionist and abstract, modern; but it was the end of a cycle. Pollock's art was modern,

abstract and expressionist, but stood at a beginning. Art-histori-
cally, it was still linked to Europe, but culturally this was American. He stripped off all the props of the old continent: prudence
and preciousness, control and restraint, intellectual and historical
references, slow genesis from beginning to end and a bow to the
public. He replaced them by American ones: speed, size, impa-
tience, unawareness, impudence, anger, tenderness.

Pollock, in his most striking contribution to Western art, drip
paintings, doesn't tend the canvas to a stretcher, and there
is no easel around. A huge canvas, the size of his studio, lies
loose on the floor, horizontal and abandoned, under the man,
who prepares to possess it. His paints come from big contain-
ers and are dissolved with a lot of turpentine. It's all against
the rules. His brushes are broad, cheap, like those of house
painters. On top of that he doesn't use them correctly, technically considered, he has them only transport the paint from
pot to canvas and then keeps them above the canvas, without
touching her. Or he turns them upside down and uses them as
dripping sticks. That causes stains all over the canvas, and a bit
on the floor, drippings exactly, as we wouldn't let a child do.
Indeed, it is painting *before* the *don't do that*, before the coming of the rules. Before the schools. And the tools! Before education. It is Nature. It is what technique serves for to overcome.
It finds man in his original state. Pollock's method is to shake
off all mankind's history, go down to the source inside and
find back the creative impulse of mere life. Pure corporeal ges-
tures, heavily sexually inspired, immediately pass from desire
to satisfaction, from idea to action. Action painting is one of its
names. Alcohol keeps the level of awareness low, of inhibition
and taboo, while psychoanalysis offers new keys to interpret
obscure behavior.

Fifty years later we are surprised to see how well these wild paintings are *constructed*, how peacefully they imitate maps of the night sky, or microbes under the microscope, how they evoke archetypal images, how classic they even look, how precious, too precious at moments. How easily *we* can accept and appreciate what in its time seemed outrageous! It certainly tells us that a man cannot—the romantic wish—shake off his civilization, only add to it, because civilization turns that wish into art. Art will absorb all that artists want to make believe it is not. It is the lesson of the twentieth century.

Jackson Pollock's name symbolizes America taking the lead in the history of Western art. He was far from alone. The generation of artists that will put New York in the place of Paris as the center of art included an admirable bunch of strong personalities, intelligent, educated, and dedicated to leave European traditions behind. It is sufficient to read the writings of Robert Motherwell, Clifford Still, Franz Kline, Barnett Newman to be convinced that there is more to be observed than the following of sudden impulses and stripping off of conventions. If it is true that several of them formed a group of Bohemians who found little sympathy outside the very small and rather alcoholic café elite, in art they led a consistent life. They were supported by two insightful critics, or call them philosophers of culture: Clement Greenberg and Harold Rosenberg. Limiting us to Pollock's case, it is evident that in his oeuvre he evolved knowingly from the art of the Mexican muralists, living Native American art, Picasso and the Surrealists. Then he leaves them behind without reverence. Though there were talented artists on both sides of the Atlantic Ocean, the difference of their historic situation is striking. And it is important to underscore that it was *not* the economic power of the American market that made the difference. Only one gallery showed these artists, for several years: Betty Parsons' on Manhattan's 15 East 57th Street. Idealistic and courageous, she could not offer the artists a living through her sales. Pollock made it, in part thanks to his marriage with Lee Krasner, a major painter in her own right. When he died he was without money or fame. Willem de Kooning and Mark Rothko began to sell when they were well in their fifties. Barnett Newman, maybe the strongest mind of them all, was not even recognized by his peers, much less by the market. The difference with Europe, then, was not material, but cultural, psychological, spiritual: culturally speaking the Europeans fought for survival, the Americans for birth, or rebirth. The European artists fought *against* a civilization, their American art brothers fought *for* one. The difference was not political either. The overwhelming majority of the American society, headed by Congress and the CIA, showed fierce opposition; these artists were politically very incorrect. They were, with the exception of Motherwell, politically indifferent or convinced anarchists. Their European colleagues, exactly on the contrary, were intellectually and politically engaged, for or against existentialism, communism, socialism, Gaullism, the list was long. They became theorists themselves. Jean Dubuffet offers a good example. The most radical of these politicized art movements or anti-art movements was the so-named Internationale Situationniste, founded in Paris by Guy Debord and Asger Jorn in 1957. Its revolutionary manifestations soon abandoned the actual reality of art to enter into the field of politics. Its greatest moment of visibility was the May 1968 uprising in Paris. By then Jorn had turned back to making art and Debord to pure theory, a most influential theory for decades to come.

In 1925, as in 1875, American artists went to Paris to be free and learn.

In 1960 European artists stood in line for a stay in New York, to be free and learn.

Very soon the American market, always alert, combined with growing American patriotism, acknowledged the pertinence and discernment of the artists and jumped on the opportunity to earn money and legitimacy. In passing they lend to the American art scene a more solid economic foundation. The great artists of the New York School would receive great commissions in the booming business districts of the great cities. The number of art galleries would grow fast. The museum and gallery directors of the Western world would do their "shopping" in New York. Abstract Expressionism had become the symbol of America's hegemony in the world.

Starting with Caspar David Friedrich's *Cross in the Mountain,* 1808, "nature" had a dynamic cultural history in the last two centuries. After a millennium of control of nature and even its rejection, its relationship with culture was inverted. Romantic art was all about the greatness of the skies, the forests and the mountains, humbling man and his pretensions. It explored the sacred awe it caused on the human senses. First as an expression of the Christian religion; soon it adventured into its pagan pantheistic and cosmic roots. One hundred years later Jackson Pollock had integrated this notion into his very body and existence. He looked upon it as the force liberating a man from creative inhibition and a tyrannical cultural superstructure. It channeled into concrete action the psychological deep sea of the soul at the crossroads of despair and enlightened ambition. We admire Pollock for having faced the abyss when it opened in front of his mind's eyes and he didn't run but welcomed it as typically human. In his crisis he turned to nature as his savior to become one with it.

Then someone (the gallery owner) asked him: "What are you doing now?
- Well, I am painting after ... nature.
- You shouldn't!
- Why shouldn't I?
- Because you *are* drip painting."
A short time after that (fictional) conversation, Jackson Pollock killed himself in a car crash.

That was the 1950-ies. In 2014 nature is in crisis and we fear: if we don't save it, who will save us? Nature has skipped from depth-psychology to biology and economy. It is our environment, and will heavily weigh on future society. Will art be given a voice? Andy Goldsworthy, James Turrell are between those who have already shown ways of approaching this nature in art.

MAJOR WORKS AND MONUMENTS

Guy Debord, *The Society of the Spectacle* (philosophical manifest)

Clement Greenberg, *Art and Culture* (art theory)

Harold Rosenberg, *American Action Painters* (art critique)

Australia, Victoria, Herring Island, Andy Goldsworthy, *Cairn*

Denmark, Silkeborg, Jorn Museum

France, Paris, Musée National d'Art Moderne, Centre Georges Pompidou, Jean Dubuffet, *Dhôtel nuancé d'abricot* (André Dhôtel with Apricot Nuances)

France, Rodez, Musée Soulages

Germany, Berlin, Neue Nationalgalerie, Barnett Newman, *Who's Afraid of Red, Yellow and Blue, IV*

Germany, Dresden, Gemäldegalerie Neue Meister, Caspar David Friedrich, *Cross in the Mountains (Tetschen Altar)*

Great Britain, London, Tate Modern, Marcel Duchamp, *Fountain (copy)*

Italy, Milan, Fondazione Lucio Fontana, Lucio Fontana, *Concetto Spaziale, la Fine di Dio* (Concept of Space, The End of God)

Italy, Rome, Galleria Nazionale di Arte Moderna, Alberto Burri, *Il Grande Sacco* (The Large Sack)

Italy, Venice, Peggy Guggenheim Collection, Jackson Pollock, *Alchemy*

Japan, Tokyo, Hara Museum of Contemporary Art, Karel Appel, *Hiroshima Child*

Switzerland, Riehen, Beyeler Foundation, Antoni Tàpies, *Writing on the Wall*

USA, Arizona, Painted Desert, James Turrell, *Roden Crater*

USA, Chicago, IL, Art Institute, Edward Hopper, *Nighthawks*

USA, Des Moines, IA, Art Center, Francis Bacon, *A Study after Velázquez's Portrait of Pope Innocent X*

USA, Houston, TX, Mark Rothko, *Rothko Chapel*

USA, New York, NY, Brooklyn Museum, Georgia O'Keeffe, *Ram's Head, White Hollyhock and Little Hills*

USA, New York, NY, Museum of Modern Art, Franz Kline, *Painting Number 2, 1954*

USA, Pasadena, CA, Norton Simon Museum, Sam Francis, *Basel Mural I*

USA, Pittsburgh, PA, Carnegie Museum of Art, Willem de Kooning, *Woman VI*

USA, San Francisco, CA, Museum of Modern Art, Robert Motherwell, *Elegy to the Spanish Republic, No. 57*

USA, Washington, D.C., National Gallery of Art, Jackson Pollock, *Number 1, 1950* (Lavender Mist)

USA, Washington, D.C., Smithsonian American Art Museum, Clyfford Still, *1946-H (Indian Red and Black)*

33. Art as Emancipation

HARLEM RENAISSANCE   LAWRENCE - BARTHÉ   1920–2000

"The problem of the twentieth century will be the problem of the color line," wrote William E.B. Dubois in 1903 in *Souls of Black Folk*. In those very years artists in France started to bring art down to a question of color. They were nicknamed the Wild Animals (*Les Fauves*), Matisse, Derain, De Vlaminck, Van Dongen, Dufy. These same artists were also the first to recognize the artistic value of African tribal art. Henri Matisse based his 1908 masterpiece *The Dance* possibly on African dance. In 1912 James Weldon Johnson wrote *The Autobiography of an Ex-Colored Man*.

Intriguing coincidences around the theme of color and art.

Already it had become clear that emancipation of the Negro could only begin within the arts. Music, dance, and poetry had come first; New Orleans and Atlanta had become centers of an expanding culture. Now the visual arts had to confirm. That happened in the 1920s in the New York neighborhood where African Americans were a majority, Harlem. The movement of great diversity and originality in the performing and fine arts was remarkable, too, for its self-awareness and the insight in its relevance. It was not only the beginning of the integration of a part of the population in a nation, but also of the integration of the arts themselves. The arts received here a *mission* from the society (or did they conquer it?), which was the elaboration of social equality through the practice of artistic values, both active and passive, production and consumption. This became typical for the twentieth century, and it is anything but behind us. Many "missions" followed the founding one of the African American.

Sometimes they were directed by the government, as was the case of the New Deal Art, and I think particularly of the Federal Farm Security Administration, sending photographers out over the country in 1935; it triggered the integration of photography as a recognized visual art and it made America its leading nation. More often the origin of an emancipation movement was spontaneous, sprouting that is from the injustice itself. The most remarkable one is that of women.

As we saw in the article on Art and Freedom, women played an essential role in the advent of modern art. The gap separating their part from the men's was still huge, as it was in the entire society. However, women were the new great deal of the century, and art was in the vanguard position. Soon women were allowed in the schools, in the academies and artist societies, in nude study sessions and drinking parties. On paper gender equality was reached in most countries after WWI; not in the reality. It shows how much the arts, too, were a male domain. And the males were not ready to give up the fortress. Progressive action in the arts doesn't guarantee progressive standpoints in social questions. A surprising illustration is given by the attitudes of the Abstract Expressionist group. The most advanced and unconventional artists of their age defended downright macho values; and while they were hardly challenged in their time, they sound downright misogynous or paternalistic in our ears. They certainly echoed unrest in the society concerning these matters, announcing change. From the sixties on it is exactly in Abstract Expressionism that we can observe how the tide was turning. Several women of the first generation, like Lee Krasner and Dusti Bongé, received already growing attention from galleries. Then women became leaders of the second generation of the movement, namely Joan Mitchell and Helen Frankenthaler. In the same years the whole American society begins to witness the rise of generalized feminism. Not surprisingly, the arts would be their symbolic battleground. The attack is here organized on three fronts simultaneously. One is frontal: women practice the arts, in growing numbers and in the same conditions as men. One reinforces the back: women occupy the discipline of art history, and partially rewrite it, changing the light it shines on human behavior through the ages. One takes over the middle field: art departments, museums, galleries, art critique and art education "fall" in the hands of women. In the arts, in fact, gender equality has reached the point such a human institution can possibly attain in any society. A related phenomenon of the last century and equally memorable is the role the arts played in the acceptance of homosexual tendencies in modern human behavior.

These grand social and cultural movements, initiated or made visible by the arts, and finally undergone by them too, causing new change, could be recognized by future historians as more relevant and fateful than the names of our now so famous artists and the ephemeral movements and interests they represent. With this in mind we would like to add a reflection regarding the emblematic emancipation in art of the American Negro.

Of all injustice in human societies the most fundamental and universal is racism and xenophobia. The American society being the first one where all the human ethnic differences met and meet, condemned to living together, racism is here more evident than elsewhere, as are the means put in motion to fight it. At the same time the American experience is likely not to remain unique, as more and more populations in the whole world are forced to migrate against their will. It is therefore that the Harlem Renaissance, moving on to the Civil Rights movement, has value of a universal paradigm.

When we submit to the very natural talent of Jacob Lawrence, attacking with magnanimity and humility, candor and lucidity, a chapter of the terrible story of his people *(The Migration of the Negro),* we admit, more than half a century after their first showing (1941) that questions of style are futile in the face of the *great cause* of the American society. Completely of his time in manner and in mood, the young Lawrence had been able to resist the art for art's sake that was so often the *little cause* of art around him. The Black population of the United States has proven of remarkable sociological unity and intuitive consciousness of its historic role by starting the story of the arts anew; that is, in the middle of the White's move towards abstraction, it rehabilitated the sense of realism and narration. It was a radical return, shared by many artists of this group, a reexamination of art's very foundations. Jacob Lawrence tells stories; and so does Faith Ringgold. Romare Bearden tells stories and so does Robert Colescott. The classical artist in their middle would have been the sculptor Richmond Barthé, the little boy from the Mississippi coast, surfing all his life on the upheavals of social change. He devoted his lifelong search to the artistic potency of the Black Male Nude, successor of Michelangelo's *Slaves* and Rodin's *Walking Man.* And the new generation tells stories in more and more daring style, Kara Walker, Kehinde Wiley, Nick Cave, Nari Ward and countless others. In the meantime, Black men from elsewhere have taken core positions in the developing art scene. Let me remind you of Haitian-American Jean-Michel Basquiat, who started as a graffiti tagger, rose to unparalleled fame in New York in only a few years, and was dead before he was thirty; and of Steve McQueen, British from the Antilles, winner of the prestigious Turner Prize in 1999, a video-artist who turned to large public films and even won the Oscar in 2014 with *12 Years a Slave.*

Barthé, Lawrence, these founders amidst many others, deplored that their fame turned back on them as being Black rather than artists. It is not an accident that they both suffered from serious mental breakdowns. Psychologically, they carried a heavy burden, and the struggle was uneven. The society resists, by inertia, bad habits, bad faith and wickedness, to the work of art that challenges the status quo. So it could happen that the exhibit organized in a University Museum of Art, entitled *Earlie Hudnall, an American Photographer*, was publicized by the PR services as *Earlie Hudnall, an* African *American Photographer*. It was a beautiful show of black-and-white silver gelatin prints.

But one day this chapter of the book will be obsolete.

MAJOR WORKS AND MONUMENTS

Australia, Canberra, National Gallery of Australia, Lee Krasner, *Cool White*

France, Paris, Musée National d'Art Moderne, Centre Georges Pompidou, Joan Mitchell, *La Grande Vallée XIV (For a Little While)*

Hudnall, Earlie, *The Guardian* (gelatin silver print)

Lange, Dorothea, *Damaged Child, Shacktown, Elm Grove, Oklahoma* (gelatin silver print)

Matisse, Henri, *Jazz* (art book, pochoir prints based on paper cutouts)

McQueen, Steve, *For Queen and Country, Britain's War Dead,* (98 pages of stamps)

Mexico, Mexico City, Museo de Arte Moderno, Frida Kahlo, *The Two Fridas*

Russia, St. Petersburg, Hermitage Museum, Henri Matisse, *The Dance*

Switzerland, private collection, Kehinde Wiley, *The Chancellor Séguier on Horseback*

Thomas, Hank Willis, *Branded Head* (laser print)

USA, Hampton, VA, Hampton University Museum, Jacob Lawrence, *Harriet Tubman and the Promised Land*

USA, Hattiesburg, MS, University of Southern Mississippi, Richmond Barthé, *The Negro Looks Ahead*

USA, Laurel, MS, Lauren Rogers Museum of Art, Richmond Barthé, *Stevedore*

USA, Los Angeles, Broad Art Foundation, Jean-Michel Basquiat, *Eyes and Eggs*

USA, New Orleans, Museum of Art, Romare Bearden, *Jazz: Kansas City*

USA, New Orleans, Ogden Museum of Southern Art, Dusti Bongé, *Circles Penetrated*

USA, New York, NY, Whitney Museum of American Art, Kara Walker, *My Complement, My Enemy, My Oppressor, My Love*

USA, Philadelphia, PA, Museum of Art, Faith Ringgold, *The Sunflower Quilting Bee at Arles*

USA, St. Louis, MO, Coll. Robert and Lois Orchard, Robert Colescott, *George Washington Carver Crossing the Delaware: Page from an American History Textbook*

USA, Washington, D.C., Hirshhorn Museum and Sculpture Garden, Robert Colescott, *Heartbreak Hotel*

USA, Washington, D.C., Phillips Collection, Helen Frankenthaler, *Canyon*

USA, Washington, D.C., Phillips Collection, Jacob Lawrence, *Migration of the Negro* (Series)

34. Art as Money

POP-ART   **WARHOL – GEHRY**   **1960 – today**

Maybe you are someone who claims not to be interested in art. Even then you'll prick up your ears when you hear about a record sale, the highest price, a spectacular auction, or the most expensive living artist (while I am writing it is Jeff Koons, but last year it was Gerhard Richter, I believe, and a year before that Lucian Freud, but he died). Never has art been valued in terms of money like in our time, and is it surprising? Money is our measure and our value. You also think that art is expensive. Well, art has never been inexpensive and it isn't today. Art materials cost a lot, and they always did; art education is long, and it always was; it takes even longer to build a reputation. Art is not like music where you are supposed to be a star at 14 and old at 24. In the visual arts prodigies are the exception to the rule. A legend has it that Grandma Moses started her career at 80 and was famous at 100. That won't happen in music or dance.

But back to money. Art expensive? Most art, certainly by living artists, is less expensive than it should be. Cheap art is bad art. Which doesn't mean that bad art is cheap, that would be too easy. But you can never pay enough for good art. What is good? That is what you have to learn to see, and you'll pay the reasonable price. In the end art is always worth the money.

Art is, of course, more than money, also in our time. Art is prestige. Social prestige. Which, as everyone knows, has no price but costs a lot. And art is rare, which doubles the price once more. The rarest thing of all is good art with great prestige. That is for the museums. In 1961, at the height of Abstract Expressionism, a master piece by Rembrandt (an artist then looked upon as a forerunner of that New York school of art) broke the all-time record for an art object in auction: $2.7 million was paid for *Aristotle Contemplating a Bust of Homer* by the New York Metropolitan Museum after a stiff battle with the Cleveland Museum. The old countries' bids were dwarfed. An all-American victory. People fainted in the public; others prophesied that this would never be seen again. We know better. Every five years until the 1990s the all-time record doubled; and no crisis has yet stopped the fever. Today even second rate living artists are paid for as Rembrandts. Prestige in a money economy can only be expressed in dollars and yens. Art is value, and money is our measure and our reward.

Why *should* art be prestigious? In those same 1960s, and already before, some young artists in Britain (Hamilton, Paolozzi), France (César, Arman, Christo) and the United States didn't see why. Why should art be old, and European, and bourgeois, and serious? Why not new and American and popular and lighthearted? And inexpensive, for that matter! A group in Italy called itself *Arte Povera* (Poor Art). Isn't *the lowest price* the slogan that makes us go? Weren't the old paintings new and modern in their own time, especially in Rembrandt's Holland, where they painted their own living rooms and kitchens and bars and burghers and therefore were beloved by the people (who then sent out Peter Stuyvesant to found ... New York), why not we? We'll send a man to the moon! And he'll send us a picture.

That was Pop-Art. Popular Art. The industrial culture belonging to everyone became the subject and object of the new art, its matter and its message. Or, let's erase the word *message*, matter is enough. The message *is* the media. No depth, no layers of meaning; the surface alone is deep enough. Our spiritual world is made of advertisement, graffiti, and billboards with neon lights. Reality is made on television and film. Promotion is our engine, success our crown, and hero worship our passion. Let our art recognize our culture, and our culture will recognize our art.

Pop-Art would become the most successful of many movements that popped up in the sixties and seventies. At that moment the spectrum of American art was wide, with imaginative and controversial artists; at one end stood the severe Conceptualists and Minimalists, exploring pure thought and form or pure painting and sculpture (Ellsworth Kelly, Donald Judd, Richard Serra, Frank Stella, Dan Flavin) on the other end baroque challengers of this austerity (Robert Rauschenberg, Claes Oldenburg, Ed Kienholz). In perfect disequilibrium they defined together the rules of what the production of art can mean in a capitalistic world (the principles of which they almost systematically and paradoxically condemned). One of the basic rules was total diversity in images, media, and aims. Unity was to be found in the way it was promoted; sometimes art evolved towards self-promotion. This was a disturbing, but fascinating happening, in the spirit of the coming world order. The art dealers, soon followed by museum curators, enhanced their grip on the artists and took a growing part in the evolution of styles, by working out the acceptance of them. The role of the New York dealer Leo Castelli became notorious, *the man who shaped the art world,* as handbooks will repeat. With his feeling for international connections the New York scene became the scene in Tokyo, London, and Paris, in Amsterdam, Basel and Düsseldorf. Museum directors and private collectors from all countries, America first, knocked on his door. It seemed that art spoke only one language, like business. The ideal to copy was the multinational firm, the New York School something like Nestlé. Europe didn't stay behind. From Yves Klein, via Joseph Beuys to Gerhard Richter, with Britain in the footsteps of Henri

Moore doubling everyone, the art scene was as diversified (or confusing) as America's; if it didn't show a unified style either, it opened great shows (Documenta in Kassel, Venice Biennale) and overall curiosity. Without speaking about the overall frustration, too. Indeed, from this moment in history on it becomes more and more random, more and more unfair or erroneous for the historian to select names, omitting others. One name must suffice as illustration for this chapter.

Andy Warhol exemplified brilliantly the new personality in art, based on sociology, marketing, public relation (PR) and a dose of personal enigma (charisma?). He was able to turn Marilyn Monroe and Elvis Presley from entertainment products into artistic prominence. Not the woman Monroe or the man Presley, but their image, even one single image. Everything the news spread as buzz was his territory, from an anonymous mortal car accident or a moon walk to widowed Jackie Kennedy or popular Campbell Soup. Not the soup but the can. Or not the can but its label. Very consistently he called his studio (in Manhattan) *The Factory.* He steered it and presided it like a CEO, attracting collaborators to work out and multiply his designs. Very consistently he worked with the ideas of repetition, mass production, and the machine, as opposed to the artist's *hand.* (How recognizable is his personal style, though, in all things he left behind!) The techniques that made this gifted *painter* well known were *print* techniques: silk screen, Polaroid, film, and video. Responding with great realism to what the public fantasy expects from the art world (drugs, sex and dollars, or in his words *Flesh, Trash* and *Heat*, titles of films he did with Joe Dallesandro), Andy Warhol became a celebrity, while his workshop became a meeting point of the city's underground culture and a starting point for new celebrities to come. Like Lou Reed, Robert Mapplethorpe, David Bowie, or Jean-Michel Basquiat.

Fame was welcomed as a central ambition of art (if only 15 minutes, according to Warhol's *famous* words). The art business transformed fame into money, and Warhol's name became the highest value in the market of contemporary art. Not for long of course. His successors in taming the market dwarf Warhol's initiatives as tentative first steps: we think of tycoons like Jef Koons or Damian Hirst.

In the second half of the twentieth century, the market conquered the world; economy was the ideology most nations paid tribute to. Art played once more its role as the visible part of the iceberg. Its place in society shifted again. Leisure and retirement, tourism and travel became parts of the normal life experience, and art was pushed forward to meet with this reality. The visual arts, old and new, joined the performing arts as to ease the conscience of the entertainment industry. Art became a holiday occupation: a museum in the daytime, with the kids; theatre or music after dinner, without them. As vacation and travel became generalized, more important slices of the national budget of every country were devoted to the restoration and maintenance of monuments and the building of museums. In return they had to reimburse the investment. London, Paris, Rome, Berlin, Istanbul, as well as Beijing, Toronto, New York City, Sao Paolo, and Mexico City are striking examples of over-populous cities that have adopted art as the advertisement and promoter of their attractiveness. What would attract a foreigner to New York (apart from business) if there weren't the Metropolitan, the Frick, or MOMA? Once landed, the foreigner would discover she missed the Whitney, the Guggenheim, or the Cloisters and she decides to come back another time. Contemporary architecture plays in this concert the first violin: who would like to miss in Paris the Centre Beaubourg, or in London the Tate Modern? Take the Pyramid of the Louvre.

Conceived by the Chinese American architect I. M. Pei, the surprising glass structure is a lobby, a cloakroom and ticket counter; but since its controversial erection on the grounds of the former Royal Palace, the number of entrances to the Louvre doubled or tripled, *i.e.* entrances to the Pyramid, not the museum. Architects have assumed a decisive part in this rapid evolution of the society. The founding of the Guggenheim Museum in Bilbao, Spain, should be considered as the reference for these spectacular enterprises. Frank Gehry's revolutionary design, as the center piece of an unequaled branding campaign by the Guggenheim firm, changed the destiny of a major city and the entire economy of a backward region. How visionary Solomon R. Guggenheim had been, when he had Frank Lloyd Wright design the first modern art museum for a modern art collection, completed in 1959. There is more happening than futuristic architectural projects. Venice, Florence, Prague, Bruges, Granada, Dubrovnik, whole living cities or their center change during the season into packed and overcrowded open air museums of ancient urbanism; reunited Berlin resembles a laboratory of contemporary art and architecture, in its middle we witness the highly symbolic resurrection of the legendary Museum Island (of old art). In all those cities, and in *hundreds* of others, art galleries abound and art auctions astound. Christie's and Sotheby's are only the most well-known of chains of auction houses that keep the market of art objects very lively, while biennales and art fairs attract clients from all over the world; there money doesn't count,

Art has become big business, and it is at the core of a web of related businesses. For governments out of politics and chauvinism, for companies out of advertisement and tax maneuvers, billions of dollars are granted to well-orchestrated blockbuster shows putting millions of people in characteristic lines in the streets under hot sun or in pouring rain. Good art is art that generates capital with capital, whatever its contents or age. Old art shines like a goldmine for poor countries, that lend or sell their treasures to the rich; but we are all poor. The art of our fathers has learned to travel by plane and by truck; specialized wrapping and shipping companies flourish. Contemporary artists prefer huge formats and fragile materials, a real opportunity for the insurance business. At the same time young artists learn techniques of public relation at least as well as of art; a successful artist of our time runs her or his business like a corporation. It sounds more surprising than it is. Renaissance artists did better when they learned to read and write some Latin. They depended on bishops and aristocrats, our artists depend on the financial tycoons and the grant systems. We acknowledge that money is a hard master; competition won't teach morality; and the artists that float to the top are maybe not of the same race as those in the Renaissance. But there is no accident, they are capable with their hands and even more with their minds, and they excel in character too. The technical media involved in the arts are not the same either: refined oil painting and flawless marble have since long been superseded by house paint, iron and cement, plastics and cardboard, photography, video and computers, installations, land art, body art, performance art, interactivity, and what not; they are usually mixed. All materials are potentially artistic now, in that sense we're back in the Stone Age. The projects tend to be overwhelming in size, and the parts are assembled by crews, supervised by the master whose name will be in bold letters on the poster, followed by a list of acknowledgments, from private sponsors to museum curators.

The Stone Age was indeed for the modern age what Rome was for the Renaissance. It is the outcome of a flux of nostalgia that has gained Western civilization since Romanticism and Symbolism.

This nostalgia longs for a proto-civilized stage of the human kind. Once called Primitivism, it is explicitly expressed in works by artists like Paul Gauguin, Max Ernst, Joan Miró, or Jackson Pollock. In the last third of the 20th century this evolved into the vision of art as myth, and the artist as the resurrection of the inspired mythmaker. Fluctuating between the absurd and the enigmatic, the superficial and the mysterious, the shocking and the healing, the destroying and the reforming and founding even of a new human being and a new society, we can include here the public *Happenings* of the radical international Dadaist movement Fluxus, and the *Actions* of the German war traumatized modern "shaman" Joseph Beuys; he famously declared "everyone is an artist."

In every epoch art responds to the dominant systems of action and thought. Subtlety is not our best vendor. The *illusion* of old has been replaced by *irony,* which is not quite understood always either. Be it so. Art is big today. Far too big for a little book like this one. By absorbing it in the entertainment economy, the society has rounded off its angles and taken away its sting. Art offers the positive news lines between wars, crimes, and natural disasters. Its impact on the society, though, is as great as that of the zoo and less than that of Disneyworld. In spite of the violence of its images and propos, contemporary art is well tolerated, but its often profound content is rarely taken seriously. That will be no doubt the challenge of a new generation.

MAJOR WORKS AND MONUMENTS

Beuys, Joseph, *I Like America and America Likes Me*, action/performance in René Block Gallery, New York, N.Y., 1974

Canada, Toronto, City Hall, Henry Moore, *Archer*
Corner, Philip, *Performing Piano Activities*, happening at

Fluxus Internationale Festspiele Neuester Musik, Wiesbaden 1962

Denmark, Arken, Museum of Modern Art, Damien Hirst, *Carcinoma*

Dubai, Abu Dhabi, Jean Nouvel arch., *Louvre Abu Dhabi Museum*

France, Grenoble, Musée des Beaux-Arts, Tom Wesselman, *Great American Nude*

France, Nice, Musée d'Art Moderne, Yves Klein, *Anthropometry*

France, Paris, Renzo Piano arch., (with Richard Rogers and Gianfranco Franchini), *Centre Georges Pompidou (Centre Beaubourg)*

Germany, Cologne (Neumarkt Galerie), Claes Oldenburg & Coosje van Bruggen, *Dropped Cone*

Germany, Darmstadt, Hessisches Landesmuseum, Joseph Beuys, *The Ströher Collection*

Germany, Tübingen, Kunsthalle, Richard Hamilton, *Just what is it that makes modern homes so different, so appealing?*

Great Britain, Ilfracombe, Damien Hirst, *Verity*

Great Britain, London, Jacques Herzog and Pierre de Meuron arch., *Tate Modern*

Great Britain, London, Tate Modern, Andy Warhol, *Marilyn Diptych*

Netherlands, Amsterdam, Stedelijk Museum, Ed Kienholz, *The Beanery*

Qatar, Doha, I. M. Pei arch., *Museum of Islamic Art*

Spain, Bilbao, Guggenheim Museum, Jeff Koons, *Puppy*

Switzerland, Basel, Kunstmuseum, Roy Lichtenstein, *Hopeless*

USA, Biloxi, MS Frank Gehry arch., *George Ohr Museum*

USA, New York, NY, Museum of Modern Art, Jasper Johns, *Flag*

USA, New York, NY, Museum of Modern Art, Robert Rauschenberg, *Canyon*

USA, New York, NY, Museum of Modern Art, Andy Warhol, *32 Campbell's Soup Cans*

USA, Sonoma and Marin Counties, CA, Christo and Jeanne-Claude, *Running Fence,* temporary installation (two weeks, September 1976)

35. **Art as Creativity**

LE FACTEUR CHEVAL   **THE IDEAL PALACE**   **1875 – today**

Art?
It is the recurrent question people ask with good reason.
Art is like a barometer. Apparently a decorative piece of furniture,
it tells us the weather to come. We need to know, it concerns us
all. Especially in times of climate change.

Why Art?
Don't ask artists. They do art because they are artists. Don't ask
the lion why it roars: because it is a lion.

So what *is* art? You insist.
Only your society can give you an answer and you can accept or
you can protest.
Your society says: art is what you find in a museum. Go and enjoy.
It also says: before you go, finish your work. People obey of
course. Most people wait till their retirement to go towards art.
They pay for a trip to see the Metropolitan, the Louvre, the Sistine
Chapel. They invite their grand-children to come with them. It is
sweet, but for the first ones it is in a sense too late, for the last
ones it is, in another sense, too early.
Art is not for children. Not more than wine or sex. Art is made
by adults for adults. The children know: art is not for them. But
your society wants you all to believe that it is just that. It presents museums before all as institutions of education. The schools
grasp this opportunity, not surprisingly. The museums have no
other choice than to deal with this, their finances depend on it.

They take great care of their educational services, who work hard to make museums less boring for the children. Art may educate, eventually; not children however, but grown-ups. Art is about life's experience, children have to live first.

Children live thanks to their *creativity*, who would deny that? Give them a piece of paper and some paint and they will make something you like. But what you like is not *art*. Some parents give them paint before they can walk. In preschool and kindergarten and elementary school teachers do the same. They call those classes art. The confusion is enormous. Children have creativity, but not art. Like children have their sexuality, but not sex. They have their drugs, but it isn't alcohol or crack. They can handle scissors and brushes and clay, but the result is not art. Because art is not in the scissors, but in the mind. Adults, indeed, need to go back *mentally* to their childhood to learn about the source of creativity (which is nature); but children need *physically* to leave childhood to learn about the source of art (which is society). So when kids do *drip paintings*, they are not the same as Pollock's. And it is a fatal error to induce this idea in children (and their parents). By the way, kids don't naturally like modern art, and that is consistent; our art is in contradiction, sometimes in conflict, with all they are obliged to adopt to become responsible citizens: clean, disciplined, obeying, patriotic, hard working, serious persons, etc. Kids strive for adulthood, and they recognize it in the control of the self and that of others; in their eyes this is symbolized by well-done figurative drawing, modeling and painting.

Kids have, in other words and quite surprisingly, kept a high and reactionary idea of art, abandoned since long by the contemporary art world. What a coincidence that in our heavily child concerned society art is placed under the umbrella of *creativity*. In short that means that the artist can do whatever. He or she is as free as a child is not even in kindergarten. He or she is an artist, who will use any material in any quantities to transform it into any form, in order to present any subject of society, according to his or her personal choices, interest, knowledge and intuition. The problem (or the luck) is that creativity is not limited to art; on the contrary, it applies to sciences and technology, to business and banking, to sports and games and before all to languages (didn't Noam Chomsky introduce the notion to our speech?!). The artist, indeed, is expected to play in all fields at the time.

How has the idea of art evolved in less than one century from nudes and still lifes in oil or bronze to this overwhelming outburst of hobby horses?

In 2013 the New Orleans Museum of Art acquired a brand new work by Will Ryman, called *America*. It features the replica of Abraham Lincoln's childhood cabin. It is made of logs and a few stones, visible on the outside, but covered on the inside by thousands of bullets, medical pills, I-phones, batteries, wires and I forget much more stuff from our polluted society. All this is hardly recognizable as such at the first look, because all is coated in solid gold paint. A quite surprising piece it is, quite moralizing too. It is absolutely wonderful for the educational crew, kids will love it, well, kind of, they will have fun; teachers may link it to subjects in about any school program, and will test the students back in class: this is pure creativity.

The *Cabin* is maybe less original than it looks. Its ancestor can be traced in a forgotten corner of France, south to Lyons, east of the River Rhône. There stands the *Ideal Palace* of the Facteur Cheval. This postman of the second half of the nineteenth century should be baptized *Father of Creativity*. As the postman of his village Hauterives, doing his daily round over a dozen miles of unpaved roads for 33 years, he would collect and bring home, in an endless harvest, simple stones and rocks of beauty and pebbles he admired, shells of snails and oysters fossilized, and sand for mortar. In the night he would stay up and assemble them into what would become a nearly 100 feet wide fairy tale "Ideal Palace". This "Temple of Nature", "Source of Life", "Source of Wisdom" and eventually the "Tomb of Silence and Eternal Rest" presents itself as a wild cascade of forms, none ever seen, but reminding one of the most exotic. It abounds in engraved references to history, religion, poetry and romantic fantasies. The whole is a moving monument to an enduring dream of the isolated obstinacy of a single human being.

The *Ideal Palace* was admired by the family and the villagers, but totally ignored by the art world. The better so. It would have been seen as an idiosyncratic performance of a hardly sympathetic provincial moron. It lacked *schooling*. But in the 1950-ies Jean Dubuffet, in the wake of Surrealist formulas, argued that being alien from all tradition, style, influence, academy, ambition and commerce, was the very definition of art. For him Ferdinand Cheval was the first artist of *Art Brut*, art, that is, free from any relation with established norms in whatever domain. Art as pure creation. In 1969 the *Ideal Palace* was inscribed on the list of France's national monuments. At that moment its legacy was clear. Half a century later it should be acknowledged as the greatest influence, consciously or unconsciously, more than Picasso or Duchamp, on the art of the later twentieth century and beginning twenty-first. It was a prophetic work. Ferdinand Cheval, godfather of (post)-modern art!

Art as the idea and apology to build your ideal palace, according to your personal views, has made its way, has its "school". Some builders were (and are!) obstinate hermits like the Facteur. Others found recognition in their society, like Antoni Gaudí and his

Sagrada Familia church in Barcelona. Some were recognized avant-garde artists, like Kurt Schwitters and his Merzbau in Hanover, Germany, or utopist architects, like Friedensreich Hundertwasser and his apartment blocks in Vienna, Austria. Maybe we can list here the interiors constructed by Ed Kienholz, by Ben(jamin Vautier), the ludic machines by Jean Tinguely and even the giant mother earth figure by Niki de Saint-Phalle. Maybe we should link to this the artist chapels, like the ones by Matisse, Lorjou or Rothko. Or a Utopia, like Donald Judd's Chinati Foundation.

With Pop-Art the idea of (sometimes extravagant) originality in materials, size, content and message took root as the new definition of art. The word creativity was invented to respect the intention and to underscore the motivation. Media were mixed. Installations were built to replace both sculpture and painting. Not the art work is invited to an interior, but the spectator is invited to enter into the artwork. Museums had to adapt. They were happy to. Since long they wanted to be more than walls to hang paintings. Their directors wanted to be more than administrators; they wanted to be part of the creative processes, even their director. Their museums needed to become the Ideal Palace of the artists (of their choice, certainly). They were the only places where many of these works worked anyway. Sculpture gardens were laid out. Inside the museums turned into polyvalent theatre stages. Simultaneously the arts were placed under the society's label of *entertainment*. Museums would invite musicians, dancers and include film in their programs. The public was rather pleased. The *visibility* of the museums grew. Which was *sponsorability*. The plastic arts and the performing arts grew closer and the public confounded them. The museums showed even more creativity than the artists alone. They promoted interactivity. They organized creative activities for the kids. They became meeting places of sociology and culture: where in the older times art was linked to poetry, now it was to (French) cuisine, (Californian) wines, (Italian) fashion, (German) fashion photography, (Belgian) strips, (Disney) cartoons and (USA) advertising. All for the show. Museums had to compete with recreation parks. It was wrong not to offer fun. They needed artists who create the buzz, the news, drama or spectacle, the ephemeral. Not so long ago museums, also the famous ones, were places of meditation, tranquility and silence, now they are places of action, interaction, and noise.

We have arrived in our own time. The very image of the situation of art and artists is biased: advertisement and entertainment cannot go against their nature.
Artists are in fact, as far as I know them, serious, very busy men and women, usually solitary workers, seen by few. Some of them are admirable organizers of spectacular entertaining events. Those have presence and the press. Some for our joy, others for our conscience.
Art however, by its own nature, I dare say, doesn't belong to the entertainment, as it doesn't belong to the ephemeral. The museums do. And so the art *world* does. For contemporary art the museum is the golden cage. Where the lion is tamed. Museums offer food and drink and a home. In exchange they silence art's voice. Or rather they keep its loud voice inside. Art seems to evolve in a closed universe today. Comparable to the wild animals in the zoo. Some artists comply, others don't. Monkeys seem to do better than wolves. Some artists fit, some don't.
One of the strong artists of the age, who don't fit, is Chinese Ai Weiwei, from Beijing. He introduced in his diverse oeuvre with conceptual overtones, targeted criticism of his government. This became very explicit when his examination of the 2008 Sichuan earthquake led bare corruption of the administration in the building of schools, where thousands of children were killed. Weiwei

expressed his concern in a chilling installation where 9010 back-packs were transformed into the most real dragon Chinese art had ever invented. Suddenly the roar of art was heard again all over the world. Thereupon the artist was arrested, sent to prison, beaten by the police, though official charges were never filed. Is this entertainment?

Museums are the gaudy frame our society has invented to sit around the art. A painting looks better in a frame. It is even protected by it from harm. But when it happens, as it happens so often, that people don't see the art anymore because of the frame, the art shakes it off. Once religion became too heavy a frame, art shook it off; once aristocratic mansions were, once the academy was, art shook them off, when the time had come.

The society decides what art is in a precise moment in history, but it cannot deny what artists do. And our twentieth century experience teaches us, contrary to appearances, that a draughtswoman or man hides in almost every artist. She and he are observing the world and draw it, period. This was true 40,000 years ago. In our time this is true too. These gifted folks are able to give us a sign of life with nothing but a pen, a brush, or a little clay, or some of them in the streets with a stencil and spray. Those humble works escape from entertainment, but continue to move us to the bone. Indeed, we humans, we are subjected to the charm, almost violently; we can't physically extract ourselves from the magic, which reveals itself in the *imitation* of life, neither from the profound mystery we call talent. Even in our time, bathing in spectacular events, some of those who did "just that", drawing, painting, established themselves amidst the recognized artists and will continue to do so. Let us honor as such, amidst many others, David Hockney, Lucian Freud, and tragic RB Kitaj in London, exceptional

Walter Anderson in Mississippi, Philip Pearlstein in New York, Avigdor Arikha and Thierry Vernet in Paris, Michael Borremans in Ghent, Antonio López in Madrid. And from New Orleans to Bristol, from Israel to the Metropolitan, everywhere, but never where you expect him, there is Banksy. Just a few random names from Europe and America, they encourage numberless others, on all possible continents, to comfort us by practicing the simple human activity that made us in the beginning and even in the electronic age remind us of what we are.

MAJOR WORKS AND MONUMENTS

Austria, Klosterneuburg, ESSL Museum, Gabriel Orozco, *Dark Wave*

Austria, Vienna, Friedensreich Hundertwasser, *Hundertwasserhaus*

Belgium, Antwerp, Zeno X Gallery, Michaël Borremans, *The Angel*

France, Blois, Ecole des Beaux-Arts, Ben(jamin Vautier), *Interior Courtyard*

France, Hauterives, Le Facteur Cheval, *Le Palais Idéal* (The Ideal Palace)

France, Paris, Grand Palais Monumenta2007, Anselm Kiefer, *Chute d'étoiles* (Falling Stars)

Germany, Hanover, Kurt Schwitters, *Merzbau,* (destroyed by bombing, 1943)

Great Britain, London, Tate Modern, David Hockney, *A Bigger Splash*

Israel, Bethlehem, West Bank Barrier, Banksy, *Children Digging a Hole in the Wall*

Italy, Pescia Fiorentina, Niki de Saint Phalle, Giardino dei Tarocchi (Tarot Garden)

Norway, Oslo, Astrup Fearnly Museum of Modern Art, RB Kitaj, *The Killer-Critic Assassinated by His Widower*

Spain, Madrid, Museum Thyssen-Bornemisza, Lucian Freud, *Reflection with Two Children (Self-portrait)*

Switzerland, Basel, Museum Tinguely, Jean Tinguely, *Grosse Meta Maxi-Maxi Utopia Meta-Harmonie*

Switzerland, Chèbres, Galerie Plexus, Artist Estate, Thierry Vernet, *Murder 05/13/1992, Rue des Envierges*

USA, Boston, MA, Museum of Fine Arts, Antonio López, *Backs (Man and Woman)*

USA, Chicago, Millennium Park, Anish Kapoor, *Cloud Gate*

USA, Marfa, TX, Donald Judd, *Chinati Foundation*

USA, New Orleans, LA, Museum of Art, Will Ryman, *America*

USA, New York, NY, Robert Miller Gallery, Philip Pearlstein, *Model with Dreadlocks and Marionette with Umbrella*

USA, Ocean Springs, MS, Walter Anderson Museum of Art, Walter Anderson, *Community Center Murals*

USA, Washington, D.C., Hirshhorn Museum and Sculpture Garden, Ed and Nancy Kienholz, *In The Infield Was Patty Peccavi*

Weiwei, Ai, *Dropping a Han Dynasty Urn* (black and white photo triptych)

General Index

Museums and monuments are listed in italics under the names of the cities or sites. Art works are listed in italics under the name of the artist, unless anonymous. In this index names are not always given in full. Dates are added to the names of all historical figures.

Made in Belgium by cultura wetteren
ISBN 9789076417189
D/2015/8746/1